# SMASH

AN ADAPTATION OF
GEORGE BERNARD SHAW'S NOVEL
*AN UNSOCIAL SOCIALIST*

## BY JEFFREY HATCHER

DRAMATISTS
PLAY SERVICE
INC.

SMASH
Copyright © 1997, Jeffrey Hatcher

All Rights Reserved

**SPECIAL NOTE**

Anyone receiving permission to produce SMASH is required to give credit to the Author as sole and exclusive Author of the Play on the title page of all programs distributed in connection with performances of the Play and in all instances in which the title of the Play appears for purposes of advertising, publicizing or otherwise exploiting the Play and/or a production thereof. The name of the Author must appear on a separate line, in which no other name appears, immediately beneath the title and in size of type equal to 50% of the size of the largest, most prominent letter used for the title of the Play. No person, firm or entity may receive credit larger or more prominent than that accorded the Author. The following acknowledgment must appear on the title page in all programs distributed in connection with performances of the Play:

Originally commissioned and presented at Carleton College
with a World Premiere at
Intiman Theatre Company in Seattle, Washington.

**SPECIAL NOTE ON SONGS AND RECORDINGS**

For performances of copyrighted songs, arrangements or recordings mentioned in this Play, the permission of the copyright owner(s) must be obtained. Other songs, arrangements or recordings may be substituted provided permission from the copyright owner(s) of such songs, arrangements or recordings is obtained; or songs, arrangements or recordings in the public domain may be substituted.

*To Tom Szentgyorgyi*
*and Victor Pappas*

"If you want to teach an audience a lesson,
you'd better make them laugh or they'll kill you."

George Bernard Shaw

SMASH received its world premiere at Intiman Theatre (Warner Shook, Artistic Director; Laura Penn, Managing Director), in Seattle, Washington, on August 14, 1996. It was directed by Victor Pappas; the set design was by Robert A. Dahlstrom; the costume design was by David Zinn; the lighting design was by Mary Louise Geiger; the sound design was by Steven M. Klein; the production dramaturg was Denise Koschmann; and the stage manager was Karen Quisenberry. The cast was as follows:

| | |
|---|---|
| SIR CHARLES BRANDON | Mark Anders |
| MR. JANSENIUS | Wayne Ballantyne |
| HENRIETTA JANSENIUS | Suzanne Bouchard |
| MISS WILSON | Susan Browning |
| LUMPKIN | William Denis |
| AGATHA WYLIE | Megan Dodds |
| JANE CARPENTER | Anne McAdams |
| GERTRUDE LINDSAY | Kari McGee |
| SIDNEY TREFUSIS | John Leonard Thompson |
| PHOTOGRAPHER | Todd Tressler |
| CHICHESTER ERSKINE | R. Hamilton Wright |

SMASH was originally commissioned by and presented at Carleton College (Professor Ruth Weiner, Chair, Theater Program), in Northfield, Minnesota, on February 22, 1995. It was directed by Tom Szentgyorgyi; the set design was by Walter F. Wojciechowski. The cast was as follows:

| | |
|---|---|
| SIR CHARLES BRANDON | David Dressler |
| MR. JANSENIUS | Clark Marshall |
| HENRIETTA JANSENIUS | Meg Higgins |
| MISS WILSON | Eric McDonald |
| LUMPKIN | Aaron Leichter |
| AGATHA WYLIE | Phoebe Henderson |
| JANE CARPENTER | Katie Weitz |
| GERTRUDE LINDSAY | Julia Wolfe |
| SIDNEY TREFUSIS | Daniel Sobel |
| CHICHESTER ERSKINE | Charles Schmidt |

NOTE: The role of the "photographer" is really not a role at all. Rather, a "body with a camera" is needed at the end of the first scene to come onstage with Mr. Jansenius. If union rules allow, use an intern or a stagehand to do the part. Otherwise, I suggest taking either the actor who plays Sir Charles or the actor who plays Lumpkin and putting him under a camera hood for this fifteen second bit.

# CHARACTERS

SIDNEY TREFUSIS — A millionaire Socialist, 30s

HENRIETTA JANSENIUS — His bride, 20s

AGATHA WYLIE — A student at Alton College, 20

MISS WILSON — The head of Alton College, 50s–60s

GERTRUDE LINDSAY — A student at Alton College, 20

JANE CARPENTER — A student at Alton College, 20

MR. JANSENIUS — Henrietta's father, 50s

SIR CHARLES BRANDON — A landowner in love
        with Jane, 30s

CHICHESTER ERSKINE — A poet and lecturer in love
        with Gertrude, 30s

LUMPKIN — A laborer at the College, 50–70

# TIME

Spring, Autumn 1910

# PLACE

**ACT ONE**

**Scene 1** — The Garden of the Jansenius House in St. John's Wood, London. A Saturday afternoon. Late May.

**Scene 2** — The Croquet Lawn of Alton College, Lyvern. A Saturday three months later. Late morning.

**ACT TWO**
The same, later that afternoon.

**ACT THREE**
The same. Two hours later.

# SCENIC NOTE

The playing area is always dominated by a carpet of green — the bright lawns of playing fields and garden parties. Pieces of light furniture and/or props indicate location: a white clothed table with a tiered cake to indicate a garden wedding reception; croquet mallets and spikes to indicate a croquet lawn. The idea is to make any radical change brisk, clean, and economical — the goal of any good socialist.

Bob Dahstrom's original scenic design for the Intiman Theatre premiere included a high hedge that curved around the back of the set. The hedge had four openings onto the playing area — which was great for clean, surprise entrances and exits.

# COLOR NOTE

The colors of the play evolve over the course of the action. White and green dominate. But the first scene introduces one drop of red. More red joins in the second and third scenes. By the last scene, red must seem to cascade about the stage — in red bricks and red flags. By play's end, red dominates the white and green. In the premiere production in Seattle, David Zinn created gorgeous costumes that perfectly complemented this scheme. One design in particular is worth detailing here. For Henrietta, played by Suzanne Bouchard, David created three dresses: a white wedding gown for the first act, a black mourning dress for the second act, and a red dress for the third act. In truth, it was the same wedding design modified in three forms, and it was stunning — especially when Henrietta marched onstage in Act Three with her recruits, decked out in blazing red, head to foot, right down to her gloves, parasol, and wide-brimmed Ascot hat. It was a sight.

## PERFORMANCE NOTE

SMASH is based on Shaw and set in a very specific world, requring a very specific style — but it is not campy. It's not a "Tennis anyone?" kind of show. It requires the fuel of real emotion and real intellect, even if it is edged in artifice. The trickiest scene is the first one: Sidney's departure from Henrietta. It should be funny, but it should be played for real. Sidney must never be flippant. He loves Henrietta. He is passionatly attracted to her. But he is torn between love and politics, and we must see that conflict, and struggle in the scene.

Another thing: these are articulate people, regardless of class or education, be they diabolists or fools. This is a verbal world, and the sound of love and politics should crackle like machine-gun fire.

# SMASH

## ACT ONE

## Scene 1

*In the Pre-Show, as the last audience members have been
seated, a boisterous version of the Wedding March Proces-
sional begins to play. As the last notes sound, the lights drop
quickly to darkness.*

*Lights bump up to reveal Sidney Trefusis and Henrietta
Trefusis, she in full white, Victorian bridal gown; he, clean-
shaven, in morning coat and striped trousers. She carries her
bouquet, he wears a flower in his buttonhole.*

*Behind them is a long table, draped in white, edged in lace,
laden with a huge wedding cake, atop which are the tradi-
tional two figures placed in the precise position Sidney and
Henrietta find themselves. On the table an array of silver-
ware, china, and champagne flutes. They are the picture-per-
fect Bride and Groom. He turns to her.*

SIDNEY.   I'm leaving you.
HENRIETTA.   *(Blinks.)* Say it again, Sidney?
SIDNEY.   I said: "I'm leaving you," Henrietta.
HENRIETTA.   Sidney, for goodness' sake, don't jest with me,
the photographer will be here any minute.
SIDNEY.   I don't jest, my sweet, I am leaving you, never to
set eyes on you again, our life together is at an end.
HENRIETTA.   *(Deadpan.)* We've been married twenty minutes.
SIDNEY.   A *lifetime*, Hen! A billion ups and downs! We've
grown old and grey, it's time to say "Adieu!"

HENRIETTA.   Sidney Trefusis, I'm beginning to think you are in earnest.

SIDNEY.   My love, my life, I *am!* And not 30 minutes from now I'll find myself upon a train out of London in hopes of driving from my mind everything about you once and forever! I am abandoning you, Henrietta! Deserting you, my bride! Exiting your orbit scarce half an hour wed!

HENRIETTA.   Are you saying you're *unhappy* in our marriage, Sidney?

SIDNEY.   Hetty —

HENRIETTA.   Was it something in the service, Sidney? Something the Reverend Mr. Prippit said? I know you're an atheist, but I would have respected your wishes if you had rather the Lord, Our Father not popped up in the ceremony.

SIDNEY.   Hetty, I am not leaving you because the Reverend Cosmo Prippit stuttered and stammered through a field of Gods and hypocrisies. I *expect* that of a minister. It's what they *do.*

HENRIETTA.   Then mother and father. Was it them? They worship and think only of me, Sidney, surely you wouldn't have banished *them.*

SIDNEY.   Like Lear or a biblical tyrant, yes! Your parents are mind-numbing, soul-choking gorgons. But truth be told — *no.* They are not my reason for leaving you.

HENRIETTA.   Then, Sidney, if this is not a *joke*, which I must say would display a peculiarly dormant sense of the macabre heretofore mercifully unknown to me and emerging now in a demonstration of timing unfortunate in the extreme; and if this is not about the tendency of the Deity to partake in the most average of nuptials held in London this time of spring; and if this is not about my parents, loving albeit soul-choking, true.... *Why*, then, Sidney, must you *leave* me? *(Beat.)*

SIDNEY.   Because if I don't, I fear socialism will never take hold in England. *(Beat.)*

HENRIETTA.   *(Darkly.)* I *knew* it.

SIDNEY.   Hetty —

HENRIETTA.   Papa said you were insane, and I see now he was right.

SIDNEY.    My sweet, listen to me: the train from Waterloo leaves in nine minutes. A hansom cab can reach the station in five. That leaves me but *three* minutes to explain to you my entire political/romantic/philosophical disposition and *one* minute to display to you the deep affection in which I hold you, an affection I wish to detail in the most physical manner I can manage given these circumstances and in these clothes. And then I am invisible to you forever.

HENRIETTA.    *(Glaring.)* Give it a shot.

SIDNEY.    Let me proceed in the dialectical fashion that harkens back to my many happy hours studying in the reading room of the British Museum:   One: I am a Socialist. Two: I am a millionaire. Three: This is a contradiction. Every half-penny I possess is stolen, Hetty, but stolen legally — my father's booty, the Trefusis Cotton Fortune! That necklace of yours was purchased with his money, Henrietta, the stains of a working-man's sweat are upon it.

HENRIETTA.    *(A hand to her throat.)* That's disgusting.

SIDNEY.    Not *real* sweat, my literal-minded darling, but the toil of countless laborers who *have* slaved and *do* slave and *will* slave on so that I may live idly.

HENRIETTA.    But it's not *your* fault, Sidney. My own family, the Jansenius family, is at the mercy of the Jansenius Trust. For thirty years it's provided us with a fortuitous bounty, but we haven't a *clue* the kinds of criminal behavior in which we're invested. Who *knows* what *we* own and whom *we* shackle! If I can't blame *my* family for what we do, it stands to reason I can't blame *you!*

SIDNEY.    Immortal powers, here is a woman who believes that the only concern my wealth should cause me is whether *she* thinks it's my *fault!*

HENRIETTA.    No, no, Sidney, it's not I alone. *Nobody* we know thinks it's your fault! If you so despise your wealth, then *give it away!*

SIDNEY.    What, to some "do-gooder" who'll only waste it in the soup-kitchen? The poor don't want bread and gruel, they want *power!* What is needed is an organization that will change the nature of the very world we know!

HENRIETTA. *(Moving to him.)* Kiss me.

SIDNEY. I am presently at the *heart* of such an organization.

HENRIETTA. Kiss me, Sidney.

SIDNEY. I am also presently the only *member* of said organization.

HENRIETTA. Close your eyes.

SIDNEY. And the truth is that the first condition of my work is to go away from you.

HENRIETTA. Sidney, I don't care if you're a Socialist, so long as you *love* me! It may be a contradiction to be a Socialist and a millionaire, but it's no contradiction to be a Socialist and a husband!

SIDNEY. That's just it, Henrietta! In my case, it is! I cannot be both! Love and politics do not mix. It's like trying to read *Das Kapital* while whistling *Tristan und Isolde*. It just can't be *done!* When I'm with you, I can do nothing but make love to you.

HENRIETTA. What's wrong with that?

SIDNEY. It is, as they say, a good idea at the time. But when I *do* escape from your arms even for a moment, it is only to groan remorsefully over the hours you have tempted me to waste and the energy you have most soundly futilized.

HENRIETTA. Then why did you marry me!

SIDNEY. *(Heartfelt.)* My dear, I had hoped marriage might *de-value* the surplus passion, as seems the case with *every* couple our blighted ruling class produces. I expected that once the shock of the actual ceremony had passed I would find passion's flame vanished in the dull roar of sanctioned matrimony; but alas my fire, post-nuptial, has been re-doubled. Looking into your desirous eyes today I saw before me a life of concentration and distraction wrestling endlessly within my breast. We love each other *too* much, Hetty; our intercourse hinders my usefulness to the cause. And so we must part.

HENRIETTA. I believe you are mad.

SIDNEY. The world is mad.

HENRIETTA. No. *You're* mad.

SIDNEY. Fine, then, I'm mad! I'm mad, I'm a millionaire, and I want to change the world! As it is, I am fit for no other calling than Saviour of Mankind.

HENRIETTA.    Then you are saying that our love, our true, fine, burning love is a hindrance to the higher calling of world revolution?

SIDNEY.    Your own happiness, Hetty, or the future of every laboring man in Great Britain.

HENRIETTA.    Is there anything I can say, Sidney? Anything I can do?

SIDNEY.    Can you assassinate the monarch?

HENRIETTA.    Not dressed as I am, no.

SIDNEY.    Then I do not think we have anything left to say. *(Sidney reaches under the table and retrieves a red carpetbag hidden there. It is the first red of the play.)* Do not track me, Hetty. Where I am going, no one can follow, what I am doing, no one must know. Plans must I make, plots must I lay. My solicitors will acquiesce to any story you should wish to circulate regarding my disappearance. When my work is done, on that day I shall return to you — and we can have a *real* honeymoon.

HENRIETTA.    *(Turns from him.)* Oh!

SIDNEY.    One thing more: I know you shall seek some soul-inspired solace once I have departed, but as to your choices? Avoid the Reverend Mr. Prippit and his stammer. I'd deeply distrust a man of God who cannot say "consummate" without threatening to swallow his tongue. *(Sidney exits.)*

HENRIETTA.    *(Red-eyed and furious.)* Ohhhhh…. Go then! Go and overthrow your silly old Capitalist system! See if I care *tuppence* for that! OR *YOU!* Or any man who *reads* again! *(Henrietta grabs up a champagne flute and hurls it to the floor. It shatters. Enter Mr. Jansenius with a Photographer, his head covered by the black cloak.)*

MR. JANSENIUS.    Hetty!

HENRIETTA.    Oh, papa! Oh, father! Sidney has left me to overthrow the British Government! *(Henrietta buries her head. Mr. Jansenius looks at the Photographer, then back at Henrietta.)*

MR. JANSENIUS.    Oh, Hetty! *(Beat.)* What did you *do*? *(Henrietta wails loudly as the lights dump out and a boisterous version of the Recessional sweeps up and covers the scene change.)*

**End of Scene 1**

## Scene 2

*The lights bump up to reveal the croquet lawn of Alton College at Lyvern, September, three months later. A few mallets and white wickets. A white, wrought iron bench.*

*With the end of the music — which has evolved from the Recessional to "Rule Britannia" — two young women in matching white school uniforms roll on on rollerskates, giggling, tugging at a large book — a book like a bible or a ledger.*

*Jane Carpenter is fine-featured and wide-eyed. Gertrude Lindsey is a bit more the junior partner and a pouter.*

*They are struggling over the book.*

JANE.  Gertrude Lindsay, give me that book!
GERTRUDE.  I won't let go of it until I've had a chance to read what she's written!
JANE.  It's not fair! She's *my* best friend, and I *insist* on my reading it first!
GERTRUDE.  *(Tugging.)* No!
JANE.  *(Tugging and pulling at Gertrude's hair.)* Yes!
GERTRUDE.  OW!
JANE.  YOU — ! *(A whistle off: TWEET!)* SHHH!
GERTRUDE.  It's Miss Wilson!
JANE.  Put it back on the bench where you found it.
GERTRUDE.  What?
JANE.  Put it back on the — Here, never mind! *(Jane puts the book on the white bench.)*
GERTRUDE.  We'd best clear off!
JANE.  Or there'll be the dickens to pay! *(Gertrude and Jane skate offstage, just as Miss Wilson and Mr. Chichester Erskine come on briskly. Miss Wilson is seated in a wheelchair, very large and im-*

*posing, a whistle around her neck. Erskine is laden with books and a note-book, his glasses slipped low on his nose. He pushes her chair.)*

MISS WILSON.   I want answers, Mr. Erskine, and I want them *now!* Where is Lumpkin, and why hasn't he brought the dreadful she-devil to me as I instructed?

ERSKINE.   Miss Wilson, I gave Mr. Lumpkin his orders immediately you issued them, the moment the indiscretion was discovered.

MISS WILSON.   "Indiscretion!" Mr. Erskine, I have never been so horrified at a student's behavior in all my years at Alton College. *Those words!* Those *AWFUL WORDS!* And on today of all days — on *Founder's Day!* If it weren't only the first Saturday of fall term, I'd cancel classes 'til Christmas! You are my first secretary in these matters, Mr. Erskine, I expect results. If a few heads roll — so be it.

ERSKINE.   Robespierre.

MISS WILSON.   What?

ERSKINE.   Robespierre, Miss Wilson. I think Robespierre said that first: "If a few heads must roll, so be it."

MISS WILSON.   *(After a beat.)* Are you comparing me to a French murderer?

ERSKINE.   *(Blinks, terrified.)* No, miss, *no! (Beat.)* Not *strictly.*

MISS WILSON.   Because Mr. Robespierre may have lopped off heads at the drop of a chapeau, but *I* am a headmistress of a girl's college, and when it comes to steely-eyed executioners *I* eat Frenchmen for *lunch! (Jane and Gertrude skate on, whistling softly, trying to nonchalantly pass behind Miss Wilson. Seeing them.)* And just where do you think you two conspirators are off to?

JANE.   *(Exchanging glances.)* Oh, why, miss, to —

GERTRUDE.   — to —

JANE.   — to study virtue —

GERTRUDE.   — and pray its practice in our married lives!

JANE.   Yes!

GERTRUDE.   Right!

JANE.   Knew it was something like that. *(Jane and Gertrude try to slip away.)*

MISS WILSON.   *ROT!* You're back-bench henchmen to that

bloodthirsty vixen *Agatha Wylie*. Support me, Erskine. You have all three of them, don't you, in your sixth form composition.

ERSKINE. *(Mooning at Gertrude.)* Morning, Miss Lindsay, good morning, beautiful morning, is it not?

GERTRUDE. *NO.*

MISS WILSON. And as it was *in* your composition class, Mr. Erskine, that the horrid *crime* was committed, I expect *you* to take full responsibility for the apprehension and summary execution of the accused.

ERSKINE. You mean *I* must be the one to punish Agatha Wylie?

JANE. *(Eyeing Gertrude.)* Oh, dear, Mr. Erskine, I shan't think *Miss Lindsay* should like that.

GERTRUDE. NO.

MISS WILSON. Agatha Wylie will be taken down off her silver peg, and that's the end of it. She has de-faced the MY FAULTS book, and after that there is no return to Paradise, no safe passage back to this, our warm and charitable bosom!

JANE. *(Eyeing Miss Wilson's bosom.)* Yes, miss, she'll be frightfully sorry to miss *that. (Lumpkin, the school handyman, trundles on.)*

LUMPKIN. *(As he enters.)* I've looked all over, mum, the ball of fire is not to be found! Were I not a disbeliever in the black arts of prestidigitation, I would say young Agatha Wylie has vanished into the stratosphere.

MISS WILSON. Have you looked *everywhere*, Lumpkin?

LUMPKIN. Well, there's everywhere and there's *everywhere*, mum.

ERSKINE. She couldn't have got off to the station?

LUMPKIN. Not quick-like she couldn't, not with that new brick wall Sir Charles Brandon's put up round his estate. 'Cause of his wall there's no short-cut twixt the school and the village anymore. It takes fully three times as long to cover ground that used to take fully three times less.

MISS WILSON. It is all the same to me if Sir Charles Brandon wants to build a new brick wall around your *head*. Lumpkin, your time at this school will be severely curtailed if you do not produce an outcome in this Agatha Wylie affair and *quickly!*

LUMPKIN. Thirty years I've worked at this school, and nary a harsh word 'til now. It's that *new man*, mum, that new man you took on three months ago who's put me in the dim light of your hard eyes.

MISS WILSON. The "new man," as you call him, can sweep a chimney, rake a path, and carry a student's portmanteau up a good five flights of narrow stairs in half the time it would take *you* to dream up an excuse monosyllabic. Mr. Lumpkin, you say you've combed the countryside for Agatha Wylie?

LUMPKIN. *(Nods.)* Combed and shaved it, mum.

MISS WILSON. Well, if *you've* looked everywhere, and *we've* looked everywhere, then where in the world is Agatha Wylie! *(A "ding-ding!" off. All turn to see Agatha Wylie — smart, bright, alive with electricity, her school uniform and jaunty hat modified for travel, enter on a lady's bicycle. Agatha wheels about the stage as the scene continues.)*

AGATHA. Morning, Miss Wilson! Morning, sirs! Morning, morning, gentles all!

ERSKINE. *(Overlapping.)* Miss Lindsay — !

JANE. *(Overlapping.)* Aggie!

GERTRUDE. *(Overlapping.)* Look out!

MISS WILSON. Agatha Wylie, come off that semi-rotorized conveyance this instant! *(Agatha continues to wheel about the green.)*

AGATHA. I want not, I shall not, I will not! How's that for compositional declension, Mr. Erskine?

MISS WILSON. Mr. Erskine, perform your duties and arrest her!

ERSKINE. I can't just *topple* her, Headmistress!

MISS WILSON. Lumpkin, apprehend the violent agitator!

LUMPKIN. Dunno, mum, I'm still nursin' a thirty-year-old hernia.

AGATHA. I cannot be apprehended, Miss Wilson. I am un-shackled, unchained, there is no return to yesterday!

MISS WILSON. *(In tears.)* Bother shackles! Bother chains! And bother *you*, Agatha Wylie! Will *someone* not halt this ac-celerated revolt! *(Another "ding-ding!" And a be-wiskered man in*

*a dapper, Abercrombie-and-Fitch version of tweed working clothes —
cap, red scarf, red socks, and yellow gloves — sweeps onto the green
on a red unicycle or scooter or penny farthing bicycle. It is Sidney,
disguised in what he thinks is a laborer's garb. But it looks very
jaunty and sporty nonetheless. Sidney and Agatha's cycles come nose
to nose at C. and stop.)*

SIDNEY. *(A put-on laborer's accent.)* Oh, hullo, miss, haven't
had the honor to make your collision. *(And Agatha topples over
to the green.)*

AGATHA. OH! *(The others rush to gather around her collapsed
figure. Sidney perches on his cycle, watchful.)*

GERTRUDE. *(Overlapping.)* Agatha!

JANE. *(Overlapping.)* Oh, no!

ERSKINE. *(Overlapping.)* Miss Wylie!

JANE. Are you hurt?

GERTRUDE. She's unconscious!

ERSKINE. *Please* don't blame *me*, Miss Lindsay!

JANE. I think she's *dead.*

ERSKINE. *Speak* to us, Miss Wylie!

JANE. Yes, *do*, Agatha, the fate of Mr. Erskine's romantic in-
clinations depends upon your resurrection! *(Agatha opens her
eyes and pops to her feet, dusting off her skirts.)*

AGATHA. I am recalled to life!

GERTRUDE. Cripes!

ERSKINE. *(To Sydney.)* Your cycling (scootering), my good
man, leaves much to be desired!

SIDNEY. *(Coming forward.)* Sorry I am, sir, but I had no call
to expect one of the young ladies to be spendin' Founder's
Day running circles round the headmistress. *(To Miss Wilson.)*
In a manner of speakin', miss.

MISS WILSON. It's not *your* fault, Mr. Mengels.

AGATHA. *(Reacting to the name.)* Who?

MISS WILSON. This is Mengels, Agatha Wylie, the new man
whose energetic presence at our school has so far by compari-
son made your co-hort Lumpkin here seem almost a da-
guerreotype.

LUMPKIN. *(Not understanding.)* Thankee, mum.

MISS WILSON. Agatha Wylie, you and I have business to

which we must attend. *(Jane and Gertrude try to leave.)* You two
— Athos and Porthos — stay put with your young gangleader!
I know you've read what she burned into the pages of the *My
Faults* book!

GERTRUDE.   But we didn't!

JANE.   We haven't!

GERTRUDE.   Barely a peek! *(Jane shoves Gertrude.)* OW!

MISS WILSON.   If you didn't *read* it, you *tried* to, and if you
didn't *try* to, you *wanted* to, and crimes of desire are still *crimes*
in *my* book! Now! Missy Wylie and her wicked wiles! In the
name of the college, its trustees and all that is good, pure,
and under my thumb, I insist you apologize for the words written in the *My Faults* book and recant!

AGATHA.   *(Arms folded defiantly.)* Shall not, will not, not my
mood.

MISS WILSON.   Very well, I didn't expect this to be easy.
Right then! Agatha Wylie: You refuse to recant the words written down by you in the *My Faults* book, the book in which
every girl must list the transgressions she has committed
against the school, her teachers, and all the forms of the good
and true. I do not expect moral force to alter either your
thinking or your actions, nor do I expect to achieve my aims
through threat of expulsion, am I correct in this surmise?

AGATHA.   *(Briskly.)* My-bags-are-packed, the-train's-at-five.

MISS WILSON.   *(Smiles.)* Right, then pack *this* in, Wylie: you
are close, are you not, to Lumpkin, our handyman of old?

AGATHA.   *(Winks at Lumpkin.)* He is my confederate and
beer-drenched Lochinvar.

LUMPKIN.   *(Shyly.)* Well, I don't know about the Lochinvar
part, but —

MISS WILSON.   *(Slyly.)* Good! I am glad of your affection!
Because if you do not recant these corrupting words — young,
smart, superior, *evil* spawn of Satan Agatha Wylie — I will have
Erskine here dismiss Mr. Lumpkin on the spot.

GERTRUDE.   Oh!

ERSKINE.   Oh, no!

JANE.   Miss Wilson!

ERSKINE.   Headmistress!

LUMPKIN. *Ouch!*

JANE. But you can't sack Lumpkin!

GERTRUDE. Lumpkin is Agatha Wylie's favorite!

JANE. If he leaves, who'll trim the lawns —

GERTRUDE. — and carry the bags —

LUMPKIN. — and sleep all day in the garden shed?

MISS WILSON. I've thought of all that. Enter Mr. Mengels.

AGATHA. Ohhhh ... Mr. *Mengels*, eh?

MISS WILSON. He's thrice the workingman Lumpkin was on his best day bright and sober.

LUMPKIN. I 'member that day.

MISS WILSON. He's fast, he's neat, he's respectful, and he costs fully two-thirds less what Lumpkin does. There, Wylie, a good, old-fashioned perplexity: your recantation, or the banishment of Lumpkin! You have one minute to decide. *(She consults her necklace watch.)*

JANE. Oh, Ags, you mustn't let Lumpkin go!

GERTRUDE. Yes, you mustn't be responsible for the loss of Lumpkin!

JANE. No!

GERTRUDE. No!

LUMPKIN. Big mistake.

JANE and GERTRUDE. *(A chant.)*
       RECANT! RECANT!

*(Erskine joins in.)*

JANE, GERTRUDE and ERSKINE.
       RECANT! RECANT!

MISS WILSON. *(Enjoying this.)* A difficult position, eh, Miss *Galileo?* What to choose? Your "new-found spirit" or your responsibility to your affections.

AGATHA. *(To the Gods.)* OHHHH! I AM UNFAIRLY TREATED! Oppressive school! Most diabolic, most crushing, most, *MOST* oppressive Alton College! It's because of this very sort of display of power that I *wanted* to write those words and be sent down! When coercive authority reaches this stage of despotic tyranny, there is no choice but violent revolt! You and this school make me want to *explode!* I had to *DO something*, Miss Wilson! *That's* why I did it! That's why I wrote what I wrote!

JANE.  But, Aggie, what *were* the offending words?

GERTRUDE.  Yes, Agatha, we're all *dying* to know!

AGATHA.  I wrote — I wrote in the *My Faults* book: "Given the oppressive nature of this institution, perhaps Mr. Marx and Mr. Engels are not as daft as one might think." *(Sidney turns slowly to look at Agatha. Jane and Gertrude gasp. In agony.)* But now ... recant? My moral force and act of rebellion — or lose good Lumpkin for once and all?

MISS WILSON.  *(A smile.)* Well, Agatha Wylie? Time's up. Which is it? *(Agatha looks at Lumpkin, who tries to appear as pathetic as possible.)*

LUMPKIN.  Me heart, miss, think o' me poor heart.

MISS WILSON.  Recantation is really such a *small* thing, Wylie. They're *words*, Agatha, just, just *words*. *(Beat.)*

AGATHA.  Very well, I —

SIDNEY.  *(Oxbridge tones.) Don't do it.*

MISS WILSON.  *(Shocked.)* I'm-sorry?

SIDNEY.  *(Back to his fake accent.)* I said: I wouldn't do it, missus.

ERSKINE.  This is your *advice*, Mengels?

SIDNEY.  Yes'm, sir. You think I can replace Lumpkin here because it appears I can work three times more than he can. But the reason I can work three times more than Lumpkin is because I've got three times less his wisdom. If I were to be given his responsibilities, I'd soon start to see the error of my ways and slow down to the proper speed — so slow as to be immeasurable — so slow as you'd think you was goin' backwards in time. By which time *nobody* in the village would want to take on his old position at the wage *you* pay for a handyman, missus. By a fortnight's folly, you'd be *beggin'* to bring back Lumpkin at *ten* times his old cost and happy to see him drunk in his shed and unable to speak the King's English afore noon. *(Beat.)*

LUMPKIN.  He's right, y'know.

MISS WILSON.  *(Red-faced, sputtering.)* This — this is a *conspiracy!*

SIDNEY.  Yes, miss, it would appear to be. And hence, I think it's not necessary, young Lady Wylie, to make such a Solomon-like choice after all, hm?

AGATHA. *(Enjoying this.)* No, not "Solomon-like," at all.

JANE and GERTRUDE. THREE CHEERS FOR MORAL FORCE!

MISS WILSON. Mr. Mengels! Depart these school grounds immediately! You have no position here any longer!

SIDNEY. Oh, let's bygones be bygones, missus. Lumpkin here's just received tenure for life. As an academic yourself you know that means the chances of his working another good, full day between now and the end of his life are slim to none. He'll *need* a, a —

LUMPKIN. A *staff*, mum.

SIDNEY. *(Smiles.)* Take it out of my earnings, mum. Mengels is just a poor orphan of the age, he don't need much.

MISS WILSON. You all think you're very clever, don't you?

JANE, GERTRUDE and AGATHA. *YES!*

MISS WILSON. *(Fuming.)* Well, I'm hardly done with you *yet*, Miss Agatha Wylie! Today is Founder's Day, and *this* headmistress still has a few tricks left up her sleeve. Someone take me to the Main House and find out what's kept Sir Charles so long on his errand to the station. *(Lumpkin makes a move.)* Not *you!* Someone with a pulse!

JANE. Send Mr. Erskine. As long as Miss Lindsay stays where she is, he'll be there and back before you can spell "unrequited."

ERSKINE. I shall return, Miss Lindsay.

GERTRUDE. *(Dully.)* I shall be hiding, Mr. Erskine.

MISS WILSON. I'll bring my *surprise* back with me. As Napoleon said, Agatha Wylie, "My army lost a battle, not the war."

AGATHA. Actually, Napoleon lost the *war* too, but quote the little dwarf if you must. *(Miss Wilson fumes, signals Erskine, and they wheel off.)* All right, team! Friends for life, right?

JANE. Of course, Ags!

GERTRUDE. Die first before we'd lose that!

AGATHA. Then follow the harridan and find out what's up.

GERTRUDE. *(Shocked.)* What, spy on Her Majesty?

JANE. *(Horrified.)* Sneak about and peer through windows?

GERTRUDE. Grovel around for dark and nasties? *(Beat.)*

JANE.    Sounds like fun.

GERTRUDE.    Right, we're off! *(They start to skate off.)*

JANE.    *(Sly.)* Perhaps Mr. Mengels would like to join us?

AGATHA.    *(Covering a bit.) Mr. Mengels should stay where he is.* I have ... duties for him to perform.

JANE.    Come on, Gertrude! We'll play at cloak and daggers and find out what's about! *(Jane and Gertrude skate off.)*

LUMPKIN.    Well, miss —

AGATHA.    Yes, Lumps, we'll find you in your shed if we need you.

LUMPKIN.    I shall be contemplatin' the terms of my permanent retirement. *(Lumpkin goes off.)*

AGATHA.    Well, Mr. Mengels, I'll wager you think I *owe* you something for saving my skin.

SIDNEY.    *(Playing with a croquet mallet.)* 'Cor, miss, it were nothin'.

AGATHA.    And I'll venture you imagine that as repayment for your efforts I'll do your bidding at some as yet unspecified future date?

SIDNEY.    P'raps so, miss, p'raps.

AGATHA.    Well, I'm sorry to disappoint you, but as you can see I'm prepared to be sent down, expelled from school this very afternoon, so I shan't think we'll have the opportunity.

SIDNEY.    I take it, miss you are not troubled to be leavin' this bucolic seat of learning?

AGATHA.    Tickled beyond giddy.

SIDNEY.    But surely Alton College is the finest school for young women in the commonwealth.

AGATHA.    Alton College teaches a stupid girl just enough to snare her a husband and an intelligent one just enough to frustrate her for life! They feed us and fatten us and put us on the matrimonial block to be bought by the highest bidder. This isn't a school, it's a marriage market.

SIDNEY.    No contradiction there in a Capitalist system. The gentlemen you quoted in the *My Faults* book would argue that marriage itself is a form of Capitalism.

AGATHA.    Marriage a form of Capitalism? Why is that?

SIDNEY.    Because marriage is an institution, and any institution in a Capitalist system is a form of Capitalism. Marriage kills the romantic spirit, miss. Revolutionaries believe in free love.

AGATHA.   Marx and Engeles say *that?*

SIDNEY.   In translation.

AGATHA.   Well, I wouldn't know. I don't know a wit about Marx or Engels.

SIDNEY.   But then how could you write those words in the *My Faults* book?

AGATHA.   Oh, our old German tutor left a copy of *Das Kapital* in our library before he left last term. I only skimmed enough of it to know it would be just the sort of thing to infuriate Miss Wilson. I've never read *Das Kapital.*

SIDNEY.   That's even better!

AGATHA.   Better?

SIDNEY.   You come by your revolutionary nature naturally, not through theory!

AGATHA.   I don't know *what* you mean, sir. All I know is that after four years at this crushing institution I can tell what's fair and what's just and as for the future they have planned for me, well ... I want *more,* Mr. Mengels.

SIDNEY.   They teach you to swoon when you should learn to say "Damn."

AGATHA.   *(Delighted.) Precisely! (She's smiling at him. A moment of mutual attraction. She looks away, embarrassed.)* And so I leave this very day.

SIDNEY.   Oh, I hope you'll reconsider, miss. I hope you'll stay just a *little* longer.

AGATHA.   Why?

SIDNEY.   Well ... seein' as we're kindred spirits.

AGATHA.   Kindred spirits?

SIDNEY.   Yes, miss. Y'see, I glean Alton College in much the same light as you.

AGATHA.   And is that why you *pretend* to be a workingman?

SIDNEY.   "Pretend," miss? Why, I'm an honest man when well-watched and have never seen the inside of a jail except four times and only twice for stealin'. Comes from bein' brought up the twelfth youngin' in a house a' thirteen.

AGATHA.   I thought you said you were an orphan.

SIDNEY. Only on my mother's side.

AGATHA. Come off it now. No workingman uses phrases such as "Solomon-like," dons yellow gloves to do his work, and handles a croquet mallet like a champion player for Westminster.

SIDNEY. *(Dropping mallet and accent.)* Ah. So you've pierced my deft disguise then, eh?

AGATHA. And "Mengels?" Wherever did you get *that* ridiculous name?

SIDNEY. A combination of two quite influential thinkers whose work I *thought you'd* know quite well.

AGATHA. Who?

SIDNEY. Mr. Marx and Mr. Engels. Marx and Engels. "Mengels."

AGATHA. A word-play Bolshevik! What's your real name then?

SIDNEY. No telling that yet, Miss Wylie, but perhaps quite soon, for I *do* think I've found in you the one comrade I've most searched for to help carry out my plans.

AGATHA. "Plans?"

SIDNEY. You and I are the rebellious product of the self-same system, Miss Wylie. Me of the beast-making organ of moloch and despair, of Eton and Cambridge, the public school; and you of exclusive girls' colleges like this very one, an institution that produced the sentimental affections and societal suppositions of a warm and impressionable woman I once knew well.

AGATHA. Oh, so it's a *woman* who's at the bottom of all this play-acting.

SIDNEY. *(Covering.)* "A WOMAN"? *HA!* Not in the least! Why is passion in a man always mistaken for sentimental mooning? Why is fire only burning if it's burning for a "SHE?" No, Miss Wylie, I have come to Alton College — in disguise, incognito — *to begin my life's great mission.*

AGATHA. It's a woman, don't be coy.

SIDNEY. All right, so it's a woman.

AGATHA. *Is* a woman? Or *was* a woman? *(Beat.)*

SIDNEY. *(Looks off.)* Was.

AGATHA.   I *knew* it!

SIDNEY.   *(Turns back.)* What?

AGATHA.   She's *dead!*

SIDNEY.   Dead?

AGATHA.   You're a *widower!* *(Beat. While Sidney thinks.)*

SIDNEY.   *(Great dignity.)* *Thank* you for not making *me* say it.

AGATHA.   Mr. Mengels, you become increasingly fascinating by the moment! But what is this great plan you have in mind?

SIDNEY.   *("St. Crispin's Day.")* Miss Wylie, we live, as I am sure you have long understood, in a society on the brink of a great cataclysm. Only a man of destiny, a man of *action* can take the conflicting forces of our contradictory dynamics and steer the raging dialectic to eloquent and righteous victory! I — am such a man of action!

AGATHA.   *(Staring at him unblinking.)* Yes you are, and what *are* you talking about?

SIDNEY.   Socialism, Miss Wylie! The new world order of Socialism! This country, this bonded isle, this bank of kings, has two roads from which to choose — on the one hand, the painful yet necessary revolution of our system of privilege, inequity, and authority; or, on the other, the bloody end of civilization as we know it. Miss Wylie, for this our England there *is* no choice: *it's Socialism or smash!* *(During this last speech, Sidney has grasped Agatha from behind and faced her out front, as if pointing her towards the new world order. His hands upon her shoulders have, however, achieved a different effect. Sidney swings Agatha back to face him. Her eyes are wide, her cheeks aflame.)*

AGATHA.   *(Swallows.)* Smash?

SIDNEY.   *SMASH!* *(Takes her hands.)* I see in this place the beginnings of THE GREAT REVOLUTION! This is the perfect setting! The great arena!

AGATHA.   For what?

SIDNEY.   *(The most natural thing.)* Why, the overthrow of the British government, of course.

AGATHA.   But, how?

SIDNEY.   *Women,* Agatha Wylie! Women! The slyer sex, the softer boot, the consorts of cabinet ministers and kings! The *future* of the 20th century! WOMEN, WOMEN, WOMEN! *(A whistle off. Conspiratorially.)* Someone's coming.

AGATHA.  Oh! But what do you need *me* to do?

SIDNEY.  I'll tell you all the details once I've found a safe place.

AGATHA.  But —

SIDNEY.  For now, there are three things to keep in mind: *Founder's Day. A large expanse of green. And a red brick wall.*

AGATHA.  Founder's Day, a large expanse of green, and a red brick wall!

SIDNEY.  *THE REVOLUTION BEGINS IN <u>ONE HOUR</u>.* SHHHH! Here come your minions! *(Jane and Gertrude rush on, without skates.)*

JANE.  Oh, Aggie, Miss Wilson has indeed something up!

GERTRUDE.  It's true! She sent for Sir Charles at the station, and they said he's on his way!

JANE.  All very hush-hush!

GERTRUDE.  He's coming here with "the secret weapon."

SIDNEY.  *(The put-on accent again.)* "Kindred spirits," right, miss? Three things to remember — I'll explain when I finds me the proper chance and place. *(Sidney exits, leaving his cycle.)*

GERTRUDE.  What a horrid man!

JANE.  What did he mean: "kindred spirits?"

AGATHA.  *(Trying to recompose.)* Never mind that, what else did you find out from the armor-plated headmistress?

GERTRUDE.  Simply that she means to crush and banish you, Agatha.

JANE.  Break your spirit and send you down for good and all.

AGATHA.  Let her try — and be *damned!*

JANE and GERTRUDE.  *Oh!*

GERTRUDE.  Agatha Wylie!

JANE.  Such words!

AGATHA.  *(Exultant.) Damn and damn and damn again!*

JANE and GERTRUDE.  *OH!*

GERTRUDE.  But if you're sent down we'll be bereft!

JANE.  We'd miss everything about you!

GERTRUDE.  Save your snoring!

AGATHA.  Don't cry, pets, I'll not be sent down before my time.

GERTRUDE.   No?

JANE.   But Miss Wilson is resolute!

GERTRUDE.   Yes, "resolute," that's the very word.

AGATHA.   Jane Carpenter, Gertrude Lindsay, as I am my witness, hear me out: when I take leave of Alton College it will be on *my* terms and no one else's. This I swear. Let her unload her "secret weapon." Fire away!

JANE.   Why, Agatha Wylie, you're absolutely scarlet! I've never seen you quite so red!

GERTRUDE.   Yes, "red," that's the very word.

JANE.   One might even suggest your cheeks had been painted with the deep crimson brushstrokes of *love!*

AGATHA.   *(Turns from them.)* "Lòve"! *HA!* Why is passion in a woman always mistaken for sentimental mooning? Why is fire only burning if it's burning for a "HE"? I'll never fall in love, *never!* I'm sworn against it, and woe to her who says it isn't so!

JANE.   Love, definitely.

GERTRUDE.   Love's the very word. *(Sir Charles Brandon enters. He is a handsome country squire in tweeds.)*

SIR CHARLES.   *(Big Twit.)* I say, heigh-ho, what?

JANE.   *(Suddenly crimson herself.)* Why, Sir Charles! Look, girls, it's Sir Charles! Why, we had no idea *you* were coming to join us today!

SIR CHARLES.   Good gosh, why ever not? Your-wish-my-command sort of thing. 'Specially *your* wish, Rainy-Jane Carpen-Tarp! *(They nuzzle.)*

GERTRUDE.   Excuse me while I become unspeakably ill.

SIR CHARLES.   Hullo, Agatha Wylie, bags all packers, eh? Rough stuff up, what?

AGATHA.   Miss Wilson is trying to break me, Sir Charles, but I have a will of iron.

SIR CHARLES.   Oh. Well, woopsy-daisy for the rest of us, then, eh?

AGATHA.   And I understand she has pressed you into helping her in these stratagems.

SIR CHARLES.   Ah, well, truth told, I'm just the errand boy: trip to the station, off and back. Took a bit of a long time today too, sort of *mob* gathered in the center of town.

AGATHA.    A mob?

SIR CHARLES.    Village green: big bunch, speakers, don't know what the grabber was, but, I say, bother, what? It's Founder's Day! Picnics along the Thames! Bonfire sing-alongs at dusk! *(Leers at Jane.) BAAAAD-MINTON!*

JANE.    *(Giggling.)* Oh, Sir Charles, you're *irrepressible! (Sidney enters.)*

SIDNEY.    Miss Wylie, I've found a deserted classroom where I can descant on my plo — *(Sees Sir Charles, spins away.)* Oh.

SIR CHARLES.    *(Brightly.)* Heigh-ho!

JANE.    Sir Charles, have you met Mengels? He's the new battalion of assistants the college has hired to aid the recently retired Mr. Lumpkin.

SIR CHARLES.    Haven't the pleasure, heard tons of course. Modern Prometheus sort of bloke, yes?

SIDNEY.    *(Looking away.)* My respects, your lordship.

SIR CHARLES.    I say, you look quite the familiar duck, Mengels. Where could I have met you before?

SIDNEY.    Er, well, I doubt a humble workingman like myself's had the pleasure, your lordship.

SIR CHARLES.    But I'm certain I've seen your face *before.* Now where in blast was it? You're — heh — you're probably not an *Eton* man, eh? What? Heh? *(Laughs through his nose.)*

SIDNEY.    *(Looking for an escape.)* Hark! I think I hear Miss Wilson's dulcet tones callin' me.

SIR CHARLES.    *(Cups his ear.)* I don't hear any —

SIDNEY.    *(Shifty.)* Oh, yes, that's her voice all right, pitched as it were so's only a humble workingman may hear. *(Sidney runs off.)*

SIR CHARLES.    Know I've glimpsed this fella's noggin somewhere before. But where? Not Eton, surely not *Cambridge,* but where the deuce *was* it?

JANE.    Well, as he's left his scooter/cycle, he's bound to be back again. *(Miss Wilson enters.)*

MISS WILSON.    Well, ladies, Sir Charles has not revealed my hidden ace, I hope.

AGATHA.  "Hidden ace?"

MISS WILSON.  Agatha Wylie, since neither moral force nor expert strategy has yet persuaded your repentance, I know I must appeal to your sense of heartfelt filial duty.

AGATHA.  "Filial duty?" I have been an orphan since I was four years old.

MISS WILSON.  Which is precisely the reason I have called upon the good services on this solemn Founder's Day of the *one* person in England whose opinion and respect you might actually crave. *(Calls.)* Erskine!

AGATHA.  What is all this?

MISS WILSON.  *Bring forth the secret weapon! (Miss Wilson blows her whistle. Enter Mr. Jansenius and Henrietta, she in widow's weeds, followed by Erskine.)*

AGATHA.  Oh, good heavens! Uncle John! Henrietta!

MR. JANSENIUS.  Agatha, what kind of difficulties have you gotten yourself into?

AGATHA.  *(Going to them.)* Miss Wilson, it's bad enough my godparent has been forced to come up from London, but my sweet cousin Henrietta has not been in a state to travel since the travails of her recent tragedy!

MR. JANSENIUS.  Now, Hetty, steady on.

AGATHA.  Is there still no news of him, Henrietta?

HENRIETTA.  *(Sniffles.)* None at all, I fear.

AGATHA.  *Such* a thing to have happened! A perfectly good husband — *kidnapped on the day of his marriage by anarchists! (Jansenius and Henrietta look down and cough together on cue.)* If only I hadn't been on the continent when you married. I've never even seen a portrait of his handsome brow. There've been no sightings these three long months?

HENRIETTA.  *(Sniffling.)* Not hide nor hair.

MR. JANSENIUS.  Not with every detective in England searching for him.

AGATHA.  Well — he'll turn up.

JANE.  Of course he will.

GERTRUDE.  Sooner or later.

SIR CHARLES.  If not later then *sooner.*

AGATHA. It's a terribly *dramatic* departure, though, Hett, you *must* take comfort in that.

HENRIETTA. "Dramatic?"

AGAṬHA. *Well!* Trucked away from the wedding reception by black-bowlered bombers with red in their eyes! That doesn't happen to a bride every day, Hett. At least it's not like he left you at the altar.

MR. JANSENIUS. A-*hem!*

AGATHA. And then you'd be forced to think up all *sorts* of ridiculous reasons to explain his absence and save your reputation.

MR. JANSENIUS. A-*hemmm!* Miss Wilson —

MISS WILSON. Your godchild still refuses to recant, Mr. Jansenius, I know your presence will make all the difference in the world.

MR. JANSENIUS. I ardently hope so, but in the meantime, Miss Wilson, the meeting of the college begins in just a moment, and as I have has just been elected to your Board —

MISS WILSON. By all means. Ladies! We shall continue our deliberations at the picnic this afternoon. (*Miss Wilson is wheeled off by Mr. Jansenius.*)

AGATHA. (*Taking Henrietta's arm.*) Oh, Hettles, the most incredible thing has happened! *Such* adventure! A *man* has appeared at the college whom I think may well have changed my life!

HENRIETTA. A man?

AGATHA. ·A *workingman!* A workingman who intends to destroy England!

HENRIETTA. (*A beat. Looks up.*) Say that again, Agatha.

AGATHA. A *laborer!* A *workingman!* A *SOCIALIST!* Oops! Here he comes! (*Sidney gallops on.*)

SIDNEY. (*Laborer's accent.*) Pardons, all, but I neglected to recover my means of perambulation, I'll just — (*Sidney stops dead in front of Henrietta, who stares dead at him.*)

AGATHA. (*Gleefully.*) Henrietta! This is the paragon of whom I spoke! Mr. Mengels, meet my most wondrous cousin, Mrs. Sidney Trefusis! Henrietta — *my man Mengels!* (*Beat. Henrietta steps towards Sidney. She offers her gloved hand.)*

HENRIETTA.　*(The Queen.)* Why, Mr. Mengels, how awfully nice to meet you. *(Sir Charles slaps his forehead and points at Sidney.)*

SIR CHARLES.　*Now* I know where I've met you! *(Sidney is surrounded. Lights dump out.)*

## END OF ACT ONE

# ACT TWO

*The same.*

*As the lights come up, Jane and Sir Charles are engaged in a game of badminton — although they carry no rackets, there is no net, and no projectile flies between them. It is a mimed exercise, and they seem to be having a slow-motion wonderful time.*

JANE. *(In the throes.)* Oh, Sir Charles! You *do* play badminton *soooo* divinely!

SIR CHARLES. *(Light exertion.)* On the contrary, Miss Carpenter, it is *yooouuu* — *(A swing in the air.)* — *ooh!* — and *your* badminton expertise that makes my own form so — *(Stretch.)* — *riiise* to the occasion! *(Lumpkin trundles on, carrying a few white chairs.)*

JANE. Oh, do mind the court, Lumpkin!

LUMPKIN. *(Confused.)* Miss? *(Jane and Sir Charles keep "playing," their efforts ever more athletic and graceful — almost missing, saving a point at the last moment, etc.)*

SIR CHARLES. We are, I fear, *sans* badminton shuttlecock and net, Lumpkin. Miss Carpenter and I have decided to improvise. Sort of the "Emperor's New Badminton Court," what? *(Swings.)*

LUMPKIN. *(Points.) Out! (Lumpkin trundles off. Gertrude runs on.)*

GERTRUDE. *(Almost hysterical.)* Conceal me, please, I *beg* of you!

JANE. *(Wickedly.)* Why, Gertrude Lindsay, from whom could you *possibly* be fleeing?

GERTRUDE. Wretched Miss Wilson! As punishment for sneaking a peek at the *My Faults* book she made me suffer a tutorial with Mr. Erskine studying the "art of the love sonnet!"

SIR CHARLES. Must've been unnerving for poor Erskine.

GERTRUDE.   I did not know the species could perspire so. At a certain point I wanted to put him in a bucket and ring him dry in case of fire. How did Medusa punish *you*, Jane Carpenter?

JANE.   *(Delivering a graceful faux salvo.)* She confiscated my badminton set.

GERTRUDE.   It's an unfair world. *(Lumpkin enters with two white chairs and a small white table. He sets them up during the following.)*

LUMPKIN.   Beggin' your pardons, misses, gangway.

JANE.   I thought the idea, Lumpkin, was for you to begin the slow crawl to workingman's oblivion. Your efforts today seem instead to be re-doubled.

LUMPKIN.   Thought I'd let the school down easy, miss. I figure if I taper off gradual, by the time I stop work altogether, nobody'll know the difference. *(Lumpkin exits.)*

ERSKINE.   *(Off.) Miss Lindsay!*

GERTRUDE.   Oh, *cripes* — *he lives!* Quick, let me in the game!

SIR CHARLES.   Righty-o, more the merrier. *(Gertrude leaps onto Jane's "side" of the "court" and begins to mime the game along with Jane and Sir Charles. Erskine enters, on the run; wearing a straw boater; holding flowers and a sheet of paper.)*

ERSKINE.   Miss Lindsay! Miss Lind — Ah! There you are! I thought I'd *lost* you, Miss Lindsay!

GERTRUDE.   *(Deadpan.)* I thought I'd lost you too.

ERSKINE.   I completed my poem, Miss Lindsay, the sonnet I foretold you.

SIR CHARLES.   A *sonnet*, eh?

JANE.   Would that be a *love* sonnet, Mr. Erskine?

ERSKINE.   By chance it is, yes. *(Erskine doesn't know quite what to do with the three of them engaged in this invisible sport.)*

JANE.   Would you like to join us, Mr. Erskine?

ERSKINE.   — uh — *May* I?

SIR CHARLES.   By all means!

JANE.   Game of doubles!

SIR CHARLES.   Here with me, the men against the girls!

GERTRUDE.   Cripes! *(Erskine joins Sir Charles' "side" and be-*

*gins to leap and swing with appendages akimbo.)*

SIR CHARLES.   Here comes a volley, Erskine!

ERSKINE.   *(Looking about hopelessly.)* I'm sor — ?

SIR CHARLES.   *(Jumping in front of him, returning the volley.)* Swing your racket, man! *(Erskine swings.)* When it's coming!

ERSKINE.   Oh.

JANE.   *Now*, Mr. Erskine!

ERSKINE.   *(Swings.)* Oh!

JANE.   Smash it over the net!

ERSKINE.   Mine again?

SIR CHARLES.   Go-ers! *(Erskine swings. Jane and Sir Charles leap and applaude as if he's made a point.)*

JANE and SIR CHARLES.   *BRAVO! (Erskine seems cocksure now.)*

JANE.   Sing out your sonnet, Mr. Erskine!

ERSKINE.   NOW?

SIR CHARLES.   Of course!

ERSKINE.   *During* the game?

JANE.   Natural joining of art and physical education!

SIR CHARLES.   Play to win, old man!

JANE.   Give as good as you get!

ERSKINE.   Well ... all right. *(As he continues to play, Erskine holds up his sheet of paper and reads, leaping and swerving with the effort of the game.)* "Ode to a Secret Love"

For G.L. by C.E.

"Nobody knows the secrets of my breastbeat. Nobody
        knows my breastbeat at all.

Nobody knows the disciples I have prayed to.
        Matthew, Mark, Luke ... and Paul.

To you, my little notebook's reams
I trust my reveries and dreams.
My chaste thoughts here set down for you,
Nobody knows my heart is true.
OOO-OOO!
OOO-OOO!

Since no one can guess, pray let us read on.
I've worn my best trousers, I've watered the lawn.
I've sang and I've danced and I've laughed and I've
      whistled,
I've decked all my halls with the down of a thistle!

Good people might think me a miserable cur,
Tho' I wear a head-warmer, a *hat* as it were.
They know not the passions that fumble inside,
Perhaps they mistake me for some other ... *guy!*

Hey, Non-Nonny!
I'm in love and I know it!
My name's not Johnny,
I'm *Erskine, the Poet!"*

*(Erskine then slams a "volley" across the "net" and collapses from the effort. He remains on the ground for a moment. Finally, he looks up.)*
Did you like it? I wrote that poem for you, Miss Lindsay. Your initials grace its dedication.

GERTRUDE.     It's like having a strain of cholera named after you.

ERSKINE.     You're a tough minded critic, Miss Lindsay, I respect that. I've been trying to include a rhyme for "Gertrude," but the only phrase I've come up with is "Squirt Food." Do you think, Miss Lindsay, my verses require a greater social dimension? Or do they demand a more burning passion?

GERTRUDE.     More burning.

JANE.     Definitely.

GERTRUDE.     Burn's the very word. *(Off. "Ding Ding." Agatha cycles on.)*

AGATHA.     *(Out of breath.)* Have any of you seen Mr. Mengels?

JANE.     We haven't spotted him since that extraordinary performance he gave here half an hour ago.

GERTRUDE.     Never witnessed a man bolt like that in my life.

SIR CHARLES.     Fella looked as if I were going to pop him! *Should've too! (Lumpkin enters, pushing a tea table and tea service, long skirts on the table.)*

AGATHA.     What do you mean?

SIR CHARLES.     Well — I was *going* to tell him where I'd

remembered him from.

AGATHA.   *(Ears up.)* *Which was?*

SIR CHARLES.   In the village! This morning on the way to the station. The street clogged with people and me late to pick up the Jansenius *pere et fille.* Suddenly there's this fella Mengels up on a soapbox shouting all sorts of nonsense.

AGATHA.   What *sort* of nonsense?

SIR CHARLES.   Couldn't make out a word, that's why I call it nonsense. Still, there was a distinctly Bastille-bound look in the eye of the populace. They get that way on Founder's Day. I was going to ask Mengels himself what was up when suddenly he dashed off and dove into the shrubbery.

JANE.   He really is too peculiar, Agatha, you mustn't go bonkers for him.

GERTRUDE.   Yes, if you're going to go bonkers for some-one, may I point out the continued existence of Mr. *Erskine.*

ERSKINE.   Sorry?

SIR CHARLES.   Who's for a swim?

JANE.   *(Jumping up, hand waving.)* Oh! Me! Me! *Breast stroke! Breast stroke!*

SIR CHARLES.   *(Eyebrows wag.)* If you insist. Agatha?

AGATHA.   Not until I've found our mysterioso.

SIR CHARLES.   Right, then, come on ladies. Erskine?

ERSKINE.   Alas I cannot swim. I fear that I should sink.

GERTRUDE.   *(Deadpan.)* Oh, pray, sir, do not let that hinder you. *(Jane, Gertrude, Erskine and Sir Charles exit. Agatha peers about for a moment.)*

SIDNEY.   *(Unseen.)* PSST! *PSSSST!*

AGATHA.   *(Looking around.)* Hullo-wha — ?

SIDNEY.   *(Unseen.)* Under here! *(The tea table shakes back and forth. Agatha lifts the tablecloth, and out from underneath pops Sidney, a pair of binoculars around his neck, his red carpetbag in hand.)* Have they gone, Agatha Wylie?

AGATHA.   How did *you* get under there!

SIDNEY.   *(Peering out front with binoculars.)* Good Lumpkin is my secret agent in this affair. His energies, once kindled, are indefatigable. You've been scouring the grounds for me, I ex-pect.

AGATHA.   Whatver gave you that idea?

SIDNEY.   "Not until I find our mysterioso?"

AGATHA.   Don't be impertinent. I only sought you out to discover why you ran away when Sir Charles was about to buttonhole you.

SIDNEY.   "Buttonhole," Agatha Wylie, seems hardly the *slanga verba*. I was a man between dual firing squads, I was lucky to escape with my whiskers.

AGATHA.   What *were* you doing when Sir Charles spied you in the village?

SIDNEY.   *(Consulting his pocket watch.)* Part One of Plan A, Miss Wylie. That Sir Charles seems to have missed the content of my oration is indeed fortuitous, but his ignorance cannot last long.

AGATHA.   *(Deadpan.)* You obviously don't know Sir Charles.

SIDNEY.   *(Takes out a map.)* On the contrary, I know Sir Charles Brandon from a time *long* before your acquaintance. From the days when we were both runny-nosed youngsters in terror of the head boys. When he was known as Charry-Bum, the Boy Brandon! That my simple masquerade has thus far succeeded in deceiving the eyes of a man I saw every day for nigh on fourteen years gives credence to my youthful conviction that he was, is, and ever shall be a practicing idiot. *(Sidney spreads out his map and takes out a gun from his pocket.)*

AGATHA.   Good heavens, a revolver! Is it real?

SIDNEY.   Of course it's real, it belonged to my father, he called it a Capitalist's subtitute for a good argument.

AGATHA.   Mr. Mengels, I think the time has come for you to reveal your notorious "plan."

SIDNEY.   Oh, you *do*, do you, godchild though you are of the infamous Jansenius Trust?

AGATHA.   What has my god-family to do with it? I'm you're comrade, aren't I? You said as much not forty minutes ago.

SIDNEY.   That was before the revelation of your ties to the Jansenius Bunch! For all I know you may even be a Capitalist spy.

AGATHA.   A spy! Very well, then, if that's what you think you won't be surprised at my sharing what few details I *do* know with Miss Wilson! *(Agatha starts off.)*

SIDNEY. *(Going after her.)* You would betray me to that two-wheeled troglodyte?

AGATHA. If miffed.

SIDNEY. This is blackmail! Is that what they teach you at this place?

AGATHA. It is by far the school's most popular course of study.

SIDNEY. Treacherous damnable girl creature!

AGATHA. *(Calls off.)* Oh, Miss *Wilson* — !

SIDNEY. All right, all right!

AGATHA. Thought you'd see it my way. As in most intercourse between a man and a woman, it is invariably in your best interests to please me.

SIDNEY. Very well, I'll tell you my plan, as long as *you* do *me* a *vital* service this very afternoon, a service which I will describe in just a moment.

AGATHA. *(Delighted.)* Vital it is, and vital it shall be performed!

SIDNEY. And you can keep a secret?

AGATHA. I can speak Spanish in code if necessary.

SIDNEY. Right, then. Pour me a cup of tea.

AGATHA. Yes, comrade. *(She pours two cups of tea.)*

SIDNEY. You remember our dialectic don't you?

AGATHA. It is one of my fondest recollections.

SIDNEY. In less than half an hour's time, as the Founder's Day speeches are about to commence, a great mass of humanity culled from my morning's work in the village will march to that large expanse of green where Alton College meets the estate of Sir Charles Brandon, an expanse of green no longer traversible due to Sir Charles' recent construction of a red brick wall. In just 20 minutes time the Alton School for Young Ladies will be an occupied encampment.

AGATHA. Occupied by whom?

SIDNEY. Miss Wylie, know this first: I am a revolutionary bent on the violent destruction of everything in England those you love hold dear.

AGATHA. Sugar? *(Offers a lump.)*

41

SIDNEY.   Please.

AGATHA.   *(Plops sugar in his cup.)* Go on.

SIDNEY.   But it has long been apparent to me that the British working class is not about to rear up against every armed authority in the commonwealth. Yet it has also become gradually self-evident that a subtler and far more diabolic revolution might take place if Socialism were to employ an army of secret agents placed deep within the very heart of empire.

AGATHA.   Secret agents? Who?

SIDNEY.   *Women*, Agatha Wylie. *Women.* If you want your cause to change the world, indoctrinate every woman you meet in it. Mothers, daughters, sisters, wives, concubines and queens. Women cannot own property, cannot vote, but they control strategic territories a charge of cavalry couldn't conquer. *(Points out front.)* Look at your schoolmates glide across these lawns: a coquette battalion, a petticoat infantry armed with dewy lips and batting eyes! One scented whisper in an M.P.'s ear is worth a thousand speeches by a hoarse-voiced radical.

AGATHA.   You think women have that much power?

SIDNEY.   I know they do — because I know the power they've had over me. Witness your cohorts and the men they dangle. If I had them won to my Socialist ways, Gertrude Lindsay would have poor Erskine writing stirring odes to the common man! Jane Carpenter would have Sir Charles renouncing his title and blowing up Big Ben!

AGATHA.   *(Moves closer to him.)* And ... me?

SIDNEY.   *(Smiles.)* Miss Wylie, with your charms, brains, and moral force the King himself would convert to Communism.

AGATHA.   *(Closer still.)* And what do *you* do with "powerful" women, Mr. Mengels?

SIDNEY.   *(Swallows.)* I used to make love to women. Now I indoctrinate them. *(He pulls away from her.)* So! If a Socialist were looking to revolutionize the future where better to plant his seed —

AGATHA.   *(Blushing.)* Oh!

SIDNEY.   *Sorry* — than in the bright, impressionable minds of the very girl creatures who will someday rule in the drawing rooms and boudoirs of cabinet ministers, captains of industry, and peers of the realm. In short — !

AGATHA.   If you're going to overthrow the British government, start at Alton College!

SIDNEY.   Our very slogan! Believe me, Miss Wylie, much revolution can be achieved by men who are not afraid of women and not in too great a hurry to see the harvest they have sown for.

AGATHA.   So what are you going to do once you've occupied the school? Blow the planet up and start all over with the rubble?

SIDNEY.   Nothing quite so Old Testament. No, my demands are these: *that Alton College teach a Socialist currciulum — with ME at the helm!* Once my army of villagers has appeared at the red brick wall they will await my signal to charge the grounds and occupy the school. I have brought with me a pair of handcuffs *(Takes them from his pocket.)* provided by a local locksmith to shackle myself to Miss Wilson's be-wheeled bunker if need be. *(They go back in his pocket. Holds up gun.)* The report from this revolver is the signal to the villagers to smash down the wall and follow me straight into the offices of the headmistress. And I shall not leave until I have what I've come to get! *(Gun goes back in pocket.)* The revolution, my dear, is nigh.

AGATHA.   Oh, revolution sounds like *such* a lot of fun! What can I do? What is the "vital service" you said you needed me to perform?

SIDNEY.   Well, for starters — you can keep Henrietta Trefusis as far away from the action as possible.

AGATHA.   *(Warily.)* Cousin Henrietta? What does *she* have to do with all of this?

SIDNEY.   Nothing at all! But her ... her *presence* here is volatile, due to the fact of her husband's ... what was it?

AGATHA.   *(Deadpan.)* Kidnapping by anarchists.

SIDNEY.   *(Sotto voce.)* Unbelievable family. *(Normal voice.)* Yes! His "kidnapping by anarchists." We must make sure Mrs. Trefusis is well out of the way when the fireworks start. To lose a love to politics is one thing; to be trampled to bits on a playing field might seem a double abuse.

AGATHA.   You think love and politics cannot exist on the

same field of battle, Mr. Mengels?

SIDNEY.    They do not exist on the same *planet*, Miss Wylie.

AGATHA.    *(At attention.)* I will do as you say, comrade! When does the balloon go up?

SIDNEY.    *(Consults his watch.)* In less than — fifteen minutes, by which time you must have removed Mrs. Trefusis from the smoking fray — *gently*, though.

AGATHA.    *(Salutes.)* Aye-aye, comrade, *sir!*

SIDNEY.    *(Boisterous.)* Agatha Wylie, if I could find a thousand men as willing as you, I might accomplish the revolution by the end of the social season! You're a woman after my own heart!

AGATHA.    *Am* I? Oh, *comrade! (Agatha kisses Sidney long and full on the lips. Finally, she pulls back and grins triumphantly at him.)*

SIDNEY.    *(Blinks.)* Miss Wylie — you have advanced your troops deep into my palace.

AGATHA.    *(Exultant.)* I love you, Mengels Mysterioso! There! *I've* said it *first!*

SIDNEY.    Miss Wylie, I'm shocked!

AGATHA.    Of course you are. Men believe women are born and bread to be raised on the Marriage Market — breaths and sighs and fluttered eyes and never admit you love him. The Great Game of "No, I Don't" when "Oh, Yes, Indeed You Do." Well, I'll have none of that! Institutions may fall today, good comrade, greens be trod upon and red-brick walls smashed down by gentlemen, but Agatha Wylie's personal revolution, a revolt of her heart and passion, the great life-force of her beating sex, begins *right now! (She grabs him.)* How's *that* for a dialectic? *(She kisses him again. Henrietta enters.)*

HENRIETTA.    Why, it's Capital and Labor, working arm in arm. *(Agatha and Sidney break apart.)*

AGATHA.    Henrietta, why — ! I was helping Mr. Mengels plan for the speeches on the Great Lawn!

HENRIETTA.    *(Smiling at Sidney.)* Well, the poor, little darling certainly *looks* like he could use some help.

SIDNEY.    *(His fake accent.)* P'raps, miss, I should be gettin' along —

HENRIETTA.   No, no, I *insist!* Don't leave on my account. I've just been at the river's edge where I could swear I heard a man speaking the most deplorable poetry.

AGATHA.   Was it Mr. Erskine?

HENRIETTA.   I'm not sure, much of what he recited seemed to come from underwater. Punctuated as it was by female cries of, "Push him down again."

AGATHA.   We are supposed to learn the sonnet form this term.

HENRIETTA.   How radical of the curriculum, then, to attempt an aquatic approach.

AGATHA.   Would you like some tea, cousin?

HENRIETTA.   Just a drizzle, my dear. I certainly don't want to interrupt what appeared to be a scene of not some little private ebullience.

AGATHA.   *(Pouring tea.)* Why, I don't know what you mean. We were discussing ... *politics*, weren't we, Mr. Mengels?

HENRIETTA.   *Were* you? I could vow I saw an intimacy that belies a fascination in parliamentary procedure. What could *you* vow, Mr. Mengels?

SIDNEY.   I'm not a man what speaks of vows, miss, so —

HENRIETTA.   Missus.

SIDNEY.   I'm sorry?

HENRIETTA.   "Missus," I'm a married woman, Mr. Mengels, "missus."

SIDNEY.   "I'm not a man what speaks of vows, *Missus*," — and though politics is not my game neither, I've more to say on that subject than those of hearts and flowers.

HENRIETTA.   I used to know a man who talked in *just* this manner.

AGATHA.   Ah, the sainted Sidney.

HENRIETTA.   Yes. The sainted Sidney. Like St. Francis, friend to all but humans. Ferrets grinned at him and budgies clamped him on the shoulders.

AGATHA.   Mr. Mengels, Mrs. Trefusis, as you may have heard, lost her husband to anarchists just three months past. He was her Apollo, and his absence is her enduring anguish.

HENRIETTA.   Oh, well ... it's not as enduring as all that.

SIDNEY.  Excuse me?

HENRIETTA.  He wasn't really all he was cracked up to be. I'd grown tired of him before his lips were dry, the anarchists must be bored to tears by now.

SIDNEY.  I am told the gentleman was a man of destiny, good and true.

HENRIETTA.  He was like two weeks in a very bad town.

AGATHA.  Henrietta, Mr. Mengels lost his *own* love recently!

HENRIETTA.  Oh, really?

AGATHA.  *(Delighted.)* Yes! She's dead!

HENRIETTA.  Don't tell me: she tried to read *Das Kapital* while whistling *Tristan und Isolde.* Agatha, I understand you're wanted by Miss Wilson at the Main House.

AGATHA.  I'm staying with Mr. Mengels, Miss Wilson can go to the devil.

HENRIETTA.  I'm sure she has an appointment all set up with him. But *for now,* she requests *your* presence in her chambers.

AGATHA.  But I —

HENRIETTA.  And I know you will not wish to argue with me, *little* cousin. I am a shattered woman, translucent head to foot, the *mention* of conflict could scuttle me.

AGATHA.  Well … *(Winks at Sidney.)* … only if you promise to come inside the Main House *just* as the speeches start on the green.

HENRIETTA.  Why, whatever you say, sweet.

AGATHA.  Then I'll be off! Don't let color raise your cheeks, cousin. And pray good comrade, sir, remember:  my *troops* are always at the ready! *Buenos Dias! (Agatha jumps on her bicycle and rides off.)*

HENRIETTA.  *(Smiles.)* Beast.

SIDNEY.  Hetty —

HENRIETTA.  No, no, Sidney, it's not with rancor I say it, just with recognition. Some people say "hullo" to their spouses, I say "beast."

SIDNEY.  I don't have time to argue, Hetty, she's smitten, not my fault.

HENRIETTA.  You're suddenly so easily *wounded*, Sidney.

SIDNEY.   I'm not wounded, but I won't be misunderstood!

HENRIETTA.   Oh, heaven take note: a man who wants *understanding*.

SIDNEY.   Well, *aren't* you upset about Agatha Wylie's crush on me?

HENRIETTA.   Not in the least. *(Henrietta plops a cube of sugar into her tea.)* Leave a *dozen* wives in widow's weeds, make Bluebeard blanch, see if *I* care.

SIDNEY.   Damnation, are you *insane*, woman? I abandoned you a bride high and dry not twelve weeks past.

HENRIETTA.   How very naughty of you.

SIDNEY.   "Very n — "! But, Lord's sake, Hetty, you should be screaming and crying and shouting loud "*J'Accuse!*"

HENRIETTA.   Oh, yes, I keep forgetting: you're a *man*. You think women are born hysterical and die of rainfall.

SIDNEY.   This is just the sort of thing I'm here to fight against, Hetty — the polite avoidance by polite society of any unpleasant truth!

HENRIETTA.   Oh, you think your flight from me was an "unpleasant truth," eh?

SIDNEY.   *(Checks watch.)* Hetty, I —

HENRIETTA.   And in fleeing you chose Alton College to ... well ... what, "Mr. Mengels?" Why *are* you here? *(Beat.)*

SIDNEY.   It's none of your business.

HENRIETTA.   *(Smiles smugly, stirring.)* Oh, I *see*.

SIDNEY.   Well, why are *you* here? And why didn't you reveal my true identity when we were introduced?

HENRIETTA.   I am here because my father thought I would enjoy a trip out of London to my old college, and Agatha's wrangle seemed a good excuse. And, as not for revealing your true identity, who says I won't?

SIDNEY.   Hetty, what's gotten into you.

HENRIETTA.   It's very simple, Sidney: I'm not the Henrietta Trefusis you left at the altar three months ago.

SIDNEY.   Really? Then who in blazes *are* you? *(From offstage.)*

MISS WILSON.   Mr. Jansenius ...

MR. JANSENIUS.   *(Off.)* I don't know, and I don't *want* to know! *(Henrietta smiles. Mr. Jansenius enters, pushing Miss Wilson in her chair.)* Ah, there you are, Hetty. *(Sidney makes to leave.)*

MISS WILSON.    Stay put, Mengels, you're party to this rabble-rousing.

MR. JANSENIUS.    *(Squint at Sidney.)* Mengels, eh? Look damned familiar. Turn round, I want to take a gander at you.

HENRIETTA.    *(Rises.)* Oh, papa, your spectacles are absolutely filthy from the train ride. Let me polish them for you. All that soot! *(Takes his glasses.)*

MR. JANSENIUS.    *(Myopic now.)* But, they're not sooty, I —

MISS WILSON.    Mr. Jansenius, forgive me for being so insistent, but if your godchild does not recant before the Founders' Day ceremonies commence, I'll have no choice but to send her down.

MR. JANSENIUS.    I thought that was what she was *working* for. You'll have to be a good deal cleverer than that if you want to break our Agatha's will. Mengels, I'm told *you* have a particular point of view in this matter. I value the opinion of the common man. Go on: tell us what you think of my ward's resolve.

SIDNEY.    Miss Agatha's will is forged in a foundry few of us in England could hope to fire.

MR. JANSENIUS.    And what foundry is that?

SIDNEY.    Injustice, sir.

MR. JANSENIUS.    *(To Miss Wilson.)* This is your *handyman?* Hetty, give me those glasses, I want to get a good look at this fellow — *(Henrietta drops his glasses and steps on them.)*

HENRIETTA.    Oh, dear. Crunch-crunch.

MR. JANSENIUS.    *(Fumes, pats pockets.)* Hetty! Now I shall have to get my other pair! Where did I — ?

MISS WILSON.    Mr. Jansenius! If Agatha does not recant —

MR. JANSENIUS.    What? You'll deprive her of an English education? She'll probably be better off.

MISS WILSON.    Better off? Raised in ignorance?

MR. JANSENIUS.    Ignorance is an undervalued commodity. Look at Hetty and me. Our family fortune is consigned to the secret holdings of the Jansenius Trust. For all I know it's invested in every sort of devilment: opium trades, white slavery, slums, sweat shops. If I perceived for certain the villainy from

48

which my wealth was derived, I might be tormented by the nightmare plague of conscience. I might even be forced to *do* something about it. As it is, my ignorance sustains a blessed innocence, and I sleep like a baby in his banker's arms.

MISS WILSON.    But surely you don't argue *against* education.

MR. JANSENIUS.    On the contrary, we all must *spell*. It's when it goes to *reading* that the danger starts. Education produces dissatisfaction, and dissatisfaction is the shortest distance to the bullet and the ballot box.

MISS WILSON.    But education is vital to a young girl! Education to a young woman is like water to a desert, like sun to shade, like baking powder to a — a —

HENRIETTA.    A wedding cake?

MISS WILSON.    A wedding cake! Add just enough and the ingredients rise to the occasion. *Too* much — and it's cake all over your face.

SIDNEY.    And you should know about pastry, yourself being a Napoleon.

MISS WILSON.    Mengels, you are an impertinent scoundrel! Mr. Jansenius, please accept the school's apologies for this menial.

MR. JANSENIUS.    Why? He didn't say it to *me*. I respect the honest animosity of my lessers. The man who gave me the advice to put my money in a trust was a menial, and because of his sly cunning I am wise enough to fear the working classes to this very day. Still: if your school can control neither your laborers nor your students, perhaps the fault lies less in them and more in the current management.

SIDNEY.    Are you suggesting it might be time for someone else to take over the reins of this school?

MR. JANSENIUS.    I don't know, and what's more I don't *want* to know. If I knew I'd have to consider my responsibility to the institution as a member of the Board, and as I have explained, I wish nothing more than to remain ignorant.

MISS WILSON.    Sir, I'll have you know my management produced last season alone the wives of 16 peers, 34 baronets, two sealords, the Conservative Party shadow cabinet, and the Consort to the Regent of Bahrein, not to mention the widows of countless American stockbrokers. Mr. Jansenius, I have given up on my *own* hopes and dreams to the management of these girls' educations! *I* could have been the wife of a baronet! *I* could have been Consort to the Regent of Bahrein!

MR. JANSENIUS.    I'll wager you could kill off your share of stockbrokers too. *(Sir Charles enters, in a silly swimming suit and boater.)*

SIR CHARLES.    I say, thought I glimpsed you 'cross the veldt! Oh, Miss Wilson, the rest of the Trustees have gathered on the lawn.

MISS WILSON.    The Trustees?

MR. JANSENIUS.    Then let's get this tribunal over and done with. Where's Agatha?

MISS WILSON.    I had ordered her brought to me not half an hour ago, but as you can see, she disobeyed me yet again.

HENRIETTA.    Oh, but I sent her to the main house, Miss Wilson.

SIR CHARLES.    I just came round the main house from the river, and *I* didn't see her.

HENRIETTA.    That's odd. She left with great purpose. *(Eyes Sidney.)* If she didn't come to you, well, I wonder what mischief she's up to? And on whose orders?

MR. JANSENIUS.    I don't know, and I don't want to know. Ignorance is bliss, as someone said — *don't tell me who, I don't want to know.*

SIDNEY.    In a Capitalist society, ignorance is more than bliss; it's a prerequisite.

MR. JANSENIUS.    *(Squints.)* Mr. Mengels, your determined candor notwithstanding, I must say there's something about your certainty and syntax I find a bit too disturbingly familiar. Why, if not for your honest workman's accent — Here, now, where is that other pair of spectacles?

MISS WILSON.    *(Looks off.)* Mr. Jansenius, would you propel me back to the Lawn of Knowledge?

MR. JANSENIUS.    But I can't see a thing.

SIDNEY.    Sir, you preach the principle of ignorance, now's the opportunity to practice it.

MR. JANSENIUS.   Very well. I'll push, and you, Miss Wilson, may navigate. Rudder as you will. Let us smell our way to Knowledge. *(Mr. Jansenius pushes Miss Wilson off.)*
SIR CHARLES.   A moment Mengels — meeting of minds.
SIDNEY.   *(Points.)* Uh, excuse me your lordship, I was just on me way back to the great lawn to — *(Gertrude and Jane rush on.)*
GERTRUDE.   Sir Charles!
JANE.   Oh, Sir Charles, there you are!
SIR CHARLES.   Good heavens, ladies, what's the matter?
JANE.   It's Mr. Erskine!
SIR CHARLES.   No harm has befallen him, I trust.
GERTRUDE.   *(Sullenly.) No.*
JANE.   He was punting our boat along the Thames, trying to recompose his dreadful sonnet when a flight of rhetoric sent his stick deep into the river mud.
GERTRUDE.   Only he wouldn't let go.
JANE.   Went right out of the boat. There he was perched upon his punting stick like a dismal flag upon a pole.
GERTRUDE.   Sinking ever so slowly towards the waves.
SIR CHARLES.   Good lord, we must do something.
JANE.   Oh, no, no need of that.
SIR CHARLES.   No?
JANE.   No.
GERTRUDE.   Eventually he went into the river.
JANE.   Where he was plucked out by a swarm of villagers on their way here to the college.
HENRIETTA.   On their way *here?*
SIR CHARLES.   But what of Erskine?
JANE.   When last we saw him, he was being carried high upon their shoulders.
GERTRUDE.   Either they've made him their king or they plan to eat him.
SIR CHARLES.   Maybe they're on their way to celebrate Founder's Day.
GERTRUDE.   They carried picks and hammers and shouted words like "KILL."
JANE.   We haven't come for help, but rather to alarm the school. *(Agatha re-enters.)*

AGATHA.    Mr. Mengels, the˙ *BALLOON* is about to go up!
*(She stops, seeing them.)*
SIR CHARLES.    Hang on, Wylers, there's a mystery afoot.
*(Agatha and Sidney exchange glances.)*
HENRIETTA.    It appears a group of *villagers* is about to descend upon the college.
AGATHA.    *(Eyes darting to Sidney.)* But why would they be coming here?
SIDNEY.    *(Indicating Henrietta.)* AHEM — *MISS WYLIE!*
AGATHA.    *(Moving to Henrietta.)* Cousin Henrietta, perhaps it is time for us return to Miss Wilson's chambers.
SIDNEY.    And I really must be —
SIR CHARLES.    Hoop-dee-doo, old man, not so fast. I want to have a word or two.
SIDNEY.    But, as yon ladies note, pr'aps I may be needed.
SIR CHARLES.    We can see anyone marching towards the green from right here. Besides, no one can cross the lawn without smashing straight into my new brick wall.
JANE.    But, Sir Charles, if the school is threatened —
SIR CHARLES.    Painy-Jane! I want to have a chin-wag with this Mengels. Saw you down at the village green this morning up on a soapbox, crowd looked absolutely red-in-the-eye! What were you saying to them?
SIDNEY.    Uh, nothin' much, your lordship.
HENRIETTA.    You take arms upon a soapbox to say "nothing much," Mr. Mengels?
SIDNEY.    I was suddenly overcome by a rush of societal contentment and felt obliged to urge said happiness upon my fellows.
AGATHA.    It *is* Founder's Day after all.
SIR CHARLES.    My groundsman says you're known as quite the local Cicero.
SIDNEY.    I have been known to string a subject to its predicate, sire, but not so's you would notice.
GERTRUDE.    Seems like pretty suspicious stuff if you ask me.
HENRIETTA.    Yes, Mr. Mengels, everything you say suddenly seems quite, quite questionable.
SIR CHARLES.    I think you'd better come clean, old sod,

and tell us what's up?

JANE.    Sir Charles, do you think Mengels is connected to this group of rabble on the march?

GERTRUDE.    They certainly *dress* alike.

SIR CHARLES.    Come, come, man, loose your soul and confess, what? *(Sidney's eyes dart. Suddenly, Agatha's hand dives into his pocket and retrieves the pistol. She points it at the others.)*

AGATHA.    All right! Nobody move!

JANE and GERTRUDE.    OH!

SIR CHARLES.    Duckers! *(Sir Charles puts his hands up. Henrietta does not move.)*

AGATHA.    I've got them covered, comrade! *(Sidney moves to Agatha.)*

SIR CHARLES.    Here now, you're not one of those *political* handymen, are you?

SIDNEY.    No, sir, politics ain't in my line.

JANE.    Mr. Mengels' line is more in the way of, well, what would *you* call it, Gertrude Lindsay?

GERTRUDE.    I'd call it love!

HENRIETTA.    "Love?"

JANE.    For Agatha Wylie! *(Henrietta smiles at Sidney. Sidney swallows and looks desperately at Agatha.)*

SIDNEY.    Say somethin', miss!

AGATHA.    Very well:  I love him.

SIDNEY.    OHHH!

AGATHA.    I would marry him by sundown, but revolutionaries don't believe in marriage, we believe in free love!

SIR CHARLES.    Good heavens, man, what have you been up to?

GERTRUDE.    Miss Wilson said he was a fast worker, and I see now she was right.

SIDNEY.    Agatha, what's got into you!

AGATHA.    I have become a committed Marxist Revolutionary! *(Agatha cocks gun.)*

JANE.    Does this mean our picnic is off?

AGATHA.    All of you, down on the green!

GERTRUDE.    But we're friends for life!

JANE.    We're almost sisters!

AGATHA.   You had nice clothes and we wore the same size, be realistic. *(Gertrude, Jane, and Sir Charles get down on the green.)*
SIDNEY.   Agatha, this really isn't the way to go about this!
AGATHA.   You want to knock down institutions, don't you? Well, this is the start.
SIDNEY.   I want to revolutionize society, not shoot girls on croquet lawns!
AGATHA.   You think you can do one without the other? Friendship is a an institution like any other, and under the definitions of a Capitalist society, *all* societal institutions are a form of Capitalism and hence to be knocked down. The government, the monarchy. Even marriage is a form of Capitalism.
GERTRUDE.   That's silly!
SIR CHARLES.   It's not silly, she's got a gun!
HENRIETTA.   *(Looking at Sidney.)* Mr. Mengels certainly knows how to knock down *that* institution.
GERTRUDE.   What, marriage?
JANE.   But a marriage is a promise.
SIR CHARLES.   And a promise made is money in the bank.
AGATHA.   Then marry a bank.
JANE.   Agatha Wylie, what an unromantic thing to say!
AGATHA.   On the contrary. *I* am the Romantic. You all confuse marriage with love. Love is capital. Marriage is a business.
JANE.   Papa says a business always loses money its first year or so.
SIR CHARLES.   And sometimes a going concern requires constant infusions of capital to keep the concern going.
GERTRUDE.   That is called investment.
HENRIETTA.   Any Capitalist or married woman will tell you that.
AGATHA.   Well, I'm neither a Capitalist nor a married woman. I am a Marxist Romantic! And a Romantic wants to be a Love Millionaire!
SIDNEY.   *HAVE YOU ALL GONE MAD!*
SIR CHARLES.   Sorry?
SIDNEY.   *The woman's got a gun on you and you're debating marriage and Capitalism!*
SIR CHARLES.   *(Deadpan shrug.)* I doubt we'd debate it any

other way. (*Lumpkin runs on.*)

LUMPKIN.   The speeches is about to start!

SIR CHARLES.   Lumpkin!

JANE.   Lumpkin, *look lively!*

GERTRUDE.   Agatha Wylie has a gun on us! (*Lumpkin looks at Agatha.*)

LUMPKIN.   Aye, miss, she does. (*Lumpkin runs off again.*)

JANE.   Oh, *no!*

GERTRUDE.   Lumpkin!

SIR CHARLES.   Lumpkin, you — ! (*Henrietta swoons to the green.*)

HENRIETTA.   *Ohhhhhhh!*

AGATHA.   Cousin!

SIR CHARLES.   Mrs. Trefusis!

JANE and GERTRUDE.   *SHE'S SWOONED!* (*Sidney rushes to the collapsed Henrietta.*)

SIDNEY.   Are there any smelling salts about?

GERTRUDE.   Call for Mr. Erskine.

JANE.   You think he carries smelling salts?

GERTRUDE.   Some men suggest the constant presence of smelling salts. He is one of them.

AGATHA.   On your feet, all of you!

JANE.   On our — ?

AGATHA.   Sir Charles, find my godfather, he's at the Trustees meeting.

SIR CHARLES.   Righty-tight! (*Sir Charles runs off.*)

AGATHA.   Jane Carpenter, go for the matron! Gertrude Lindsay, alert the chemist!

GERTRUDE.   It's a trick!

JANE.   Gertrude!

GERTRUDE.   She's going to shoot us in the back!

AGATHA.   Hop to it, there's no time to lose! (*Jane and Gertrude scurry off.*) Is she alive?

SIDNEY.   She's breathing shallowly, but then she always did.

AGATHA.   "Always?"

SIDNEY.   Agatha Wylie, the villagers will be at the wall any moment now. Tell them to wait. I cannot lead them until we know Mrs. Trefusis is all right. This is *just* what I had hoped

55

to guard against! Hetty, you are my undoing yet again!

AGATHA.  "Hetty?"

SIDNEY.  Advance your troops, woman!

AGATHA.  Very well, comrade. *(Agatha places the revolver on the tea table and rushes off.)*

SIDNEY.  Oh, Hetty, Hetty, I *knew* you were a wilting swan! Why did you ever come down here! Come back to me, my darling! Please, *please* come back to me! *(Henrietta's eyes are still closed, her face impassive.) OH, HETTY! (Sidney kisses her full on the lips. Her arms come around his neck.)*

HENRIETTA.  OH, SIDNEY!

SIDNEY.  *(Leaps up.)* AH-HA! I knew you were pretending, you great silly cow!

HENRIETTA.  *(Stands.)* Well, I got rid of them, didn't I? Oh, *kiss* me again, Sidney! *(She grabs him.)* My dearest, I've missed you so! Do you know what it cost my heart to pretend I didn't recognize you, pretend I didn't care?

SIDNEY.  Hush, darling, now unhand me, I have to get you away from here!

HENRIETTA.  What are you doing, Sidney? What horrible danger have you put yourself in?

SIDNEY.  My sweet, there is no danger.

HENRIETTA.  You made my cousin pull a gun on us!

SIDNEY.  It happens in the best of families. Now, come on!

HENRIETTA.  Oh, Sidney, I hate you so! You were making love to Agatha Wylie! You have no right to make love to anyone but me!

SIDNEY.  Ah-*ha!* I *knew* you were jealous! Property rights, Hett, you are angry because Agatha has infringed on your *monopoly!*

HENRIETTA.  Oh, you huge child, it's not monopoly, it's not politics, it's *love*, Sidney, *love*, and the fact of the matter is you don't love *me!* *(She turns from him.)*

SIDNEY.  Don't *love* you? Hetty, I love you so much it's *alarming!*

HENRIETTA.  You *do?*

SIDNEY.  Yes!

HENRIETTA.  You *DO?*

SIDNEY.    *YES!* Hetty, you are the bright sun of my senses, the flame of my every desire! I feel my heart and brain within your smile, my thoughts and my soul within your voice. I miss you, Hetty. I miss the both of us. And when we part today, I'll miss us both again. *(Beat. Henrietta turns to look at him.)*
HENRIETTA.    *(A shift in tone.)* Sidney, are you in trouble? What you're about to do, does it place you deep in danger?
SIDNEY.    In harm's way, but never Achilles I as long as there is you.
HENRIETTA.    But *today*, Sidney, what are you planning *to-day?*
SIDNEY.    Take no concern, my dove, just close your eyes and think of Sidney.
HENRIETTA.    But if you don't tell me *why* I'm not to worry, I'll go mad inventing nightmare after nightmare to befall you!
SIDNEY.    Very well, petal. In just moments the village of Lyvern will occupy Alton College in the first action of my revolution. Once occupied, I will present my demands to the Trustees.
HENRIETTA.    Which are?
SIDNEY.    That they give the college to me.
HENRIETTA.    You would do anything to lecture women, wouldn't you?
SIDNEY.    Teach them how to drink their tea, and their hearts and minds will follow.
HENRIETTA.    And how did you get the village to march upon Alton College?
SIDNEY.    Promise not to tell?
HENRIETTA.    Yes.
SIDNEY.    I *paid* them each five pounds.
HENRIETTA.    You *paid* them? A *purchased* revolt? *(Sidney takes out the handcuffs from his pocket.)*
SIDNEY.    I even purchased handcuffs to *shackle* me to the school. The locksmith is a particular convert of mine. Since I got him to thinking along Socialist lines he never sees a gentleman without feeling inclined to heave a brick at him. *(Henrietta takes the handcuffs.)*
HENRIETTA.    But you've used *money* to start the revolution!

SIDNEY.   I even tipped them to sing "The Internationale"! They shall storm the barricades waving a thousand red flags! Their signal is the gunshot. My father's ill-gotten loot has purchased the first chink in Great Britain's wall!

HENRIETTA.   And that's it? That's your plan?

SIDNEY.   In a bombshell.

HENRIETTA.   None other?

SIDNEY.   Not for today. Now, kiss me, and let's go!

HENRIETTA.   *(Turns to him.)* Close your eyes.

SIDNEY.   *(Eyes closed.)* Very well.

HENRIETTA.   *(A different kind of smile.)* Are they shut tight?

SIDNEY.   Hmmmmm.

HENRIETTA.   Right then! *(Henrietta slaps one bracelet of the handcuff on Sidney's wrist. Sidney's eyes open.)*

SIDNEY.   Hetty, what — ? *(Henrietta cuffs the other bracelet of the handcuffs to the tea table.)*

HENRIETTA.   *(A savage glint.)* So you want to kiss me *now*, eh, *petal*?

SIDNEY.   Henrietta, stop playing at tigers, I've a revolution to commence!

HENRIETTA.   Command your army from the tea table! Issue orders with a scone and biscuit!

SIDNEY.   Henrietta, I believe you have deceived me!

HENRIETTA.   Frailty, thy name is Sidney. *(Henrietta takes the binoculars from around his neck. They snap off.)*

SIDNEY.   Oww! Hetty! You were making love to me simply to gain advantage!

HENRIETTA.   *(Growing fury.)* Well, I learnt it at my husband's knee. You want to know how your wilting swan passed these last three *shuddering* months?

SIDNEY.   Hetty —

HENRIETTA.   *(Gaining real force.)* First, I contemplated the gas. *Oh, yes, Sidney! I DID!* But then I thought "NO. It will only make him play the martyr and lend tragic romance to his vile cause." Then I considered joining a convent and taking the vow of chastity but suddenly recalled that long weekend we spent in Walthamstow and thought the better of it. Last I became jealous.

SIDNEY.   Jealous! Hetty, there was no co-respondent!

HENRIETTA.   Oh, yes, there was! I had my rival! But she was no flesh and blood DuBarry! She was more than deep green eyes and a pouting lip and hair that you could sit on. She was an IDEA! But a trollop homewrecker nonetheless! So I did what *any* spurned wife would do, any wife who'd not lost her self-respect and fighting spirit. I *tracked* the strumpet to her lair, her den of sin, and you know where I found your mistress's boudoir? IN THE READING ROOM OF THE BRITISH MUSEUM! And there I studied Marx and Engels, the whole she-bang, the volume complete — IN ENGLISH AND IN GERMAN! Dozens of books, thousands of pages, sleepless nights and red my eyes, and do you know what I discovered about your concubine?

SIDNEY.   What?

HENRIETTA.   It's bollocks!

SIDNEY.   *(Gasps, horrified.)* AHHH!

HENRIETTA.   Bollocks! Marx and Engels, they're *shams!* Frauds and charlatans, the pair of them!

SIDNEY.   BLASPHEMY!

HENRIETTA.   Oh, they're bright enough and smart enough, but their ideas for *changing* things! Socialism may be a wonderful way of analyzing society, but it's a terrible way to *run* one. In all their diagrams for Utopia, they leave out the essential fact that *human beings* will be involved! Men and women who want other than food and clothes and certainly *more* than equality. For affection is not equal. Pain is not equal. And neither is revenge. And now that I know what your great *plan* is — *(Henrietta picks up the binoculars.)*

SIDNEY.   *(Tugging at his handcuffs.)* Hetty, what are you doing — ?

HENRIETTA.   *(Peering out front through the binoculars.)* Oh, *look!* It seems a happy clutch of *villagers* has gathered at the wall!

SIDNEY.   Hetty, unchain me, I implore you! The key is in my — *(Mr. Jansenius enters, now wearing glasses.)*

MR. JANSENIUS.   My dear, Agatha said you had fallen ill, I — *(Mr. Jansenius squints at Sidney.)* Good Lord! It's — it's — !

HENRIETTA.   *(Steering him from Sidney.)* Come along, papa, we've some business with the Trustees.

MR. JANSENIUS.    Who is that — ?

HENRIETTA.    Just a harmless madman fond of disguising himself so as to frighten the slower children.

MR. JANSENIUS.    But — !

HENRIETTA.    Yes, looks just like Sidney, doesn't he?

MR. JANSENIUS.    But surely it *is* — !

HENRIETTA.    *(Takes her father's glasses.)* It's just your spectacles, papa. See? *(She hurls them over the hedge offstage.)* OOOPS! Now off we go!

MR. JANSENIUS.    *(Confused.)* Wha —

SIDNEY.    Henrietta, what are you going to *do?*

HENRIETTA.    You took Agatha Wylie and made her into a revolutionary terrorist all in a morning's work. Well, we'll see where her heart and mind is by day's end! I'm not finished with you *yet*, Mr. Mengels! Not finished, comrade, by a longshot! *(Henrietta takes the gun and marches off with Mr. Jansenius.)*

SIDNEY.    Henrietta! Henrietta, uncuff me this instant! *(Gertrude rushes on.)*

GERTRUDE.    Hide me! Hide me!

SIDNEY.    Miss Lindsay!

GERTRUDE.    *(Points at tea table.)* SANCTUARY!

SIDNEY.    Sanctuary, quite, yes, I — *(Gertrude crawls under the tea table.)*

GERTRUDE.    *(Snarls.)* Don't move about so!

SIDNEY.    I'll stay still happily, if only you'll reach into my pocket for a key —

GERTRUDE.    *(Under table skirts.)* BE QUIET!

ERSKINE.    *(Off.)* Miss Lindsay! *(Erskine rushes on, his clothes drenched, his poem wet and limp in his hand.)* Mr. Mengels, have you seen Miss Lindsay?

SIDNEY.    I — *(A hand slaps him from under the cloth.)* NO! I — I haven't, but if you'd do me the favor of reaching into my pock —

ERSKINE.    *(Looking around, panicked.)* I must find her, she has a false impression of my rhyme-scheme! *(Erskine runs off.)*

SIDNEY.    But Mr. Erskine — ! *(Gertrude pops out again.)*

GERTRUDE.    Thanks awfully, got to run!

SIDNEY.    But Miss Lindsay — *(Gertrude runs off, just as Jane has run on.)* Miss Carpenter, thank *God* you've arrived! *Will* you unshackle me? *(Jane slaps Sidney.)*

JANE.    THERE! That's for what you've done to Agatha Wylie!

SIDNEY.    I?

JANE.    I saw you kissing Mrs. Trefusis! To be a laborer washing the weak brain of an impressionable young girl is one thing, but to turn one's back and start immediately making love to a near-widow practically *twenty-three* years of old age is an act of such appalling treason I can only slap you again! *(Jane slaps him again.)*

SIDNEY.    Ow! But Miss Carpen — *(Jane runs off, crying. Sir Charles runs on.)*

SIR CHARLES.    I say, Jane — !

SIDNEY.    I've been shackled by Mrs. Trefusis, your lordship, prithee, undo me!

SIR CHARLES.    Oh, don't know as I can do *that;* Mrs. T's husband was kidnapped by anarchists, in my book that makes her every action pretty much above reproach.

SIDNEY.    *(Losing his temper and his accent.)* CHARRY-BUM BRANDON, YOU INSUFFERABLE TWIT, GET THE KEYS FROM MY POCKET AND UNLOCK THESE HANDCUFFS!

SIR CHARLES.    *(Blinks.)* Good lord. Sidders Smilash. The Boy Trefusis. I *knew* I recognized you! I wouldn't unchain you if the fate of England itself depended on it. *(Lumpkin comes on. He carries something at his side.)*

SIDNEY.    Lumpkin! At long last Lumpkin! My dear confederate, unchain me!

LUMPKIN.    Sorry, sir, Mrs. Trefusis paid me not to.

SIDNEY.    Infernal Capital!

LUMPKIN.    She also paid me to do this. *(Lumpkin reveals that he is holding the pistol and fires it into the air.)*

SIR CHARLES.    *(Looking out.)* Heigh-ho! *(Voices singing louder.)* The villagers are coming across the green. They're smashing through my wall.

SIDNEY.    Four hundred of the proletariat, good and true!

SIR CHARLES.    They're drunk as Irishmen!

SIDNEY.    What do you mean? That is the might of the *people* crossing that lawn! Singing "The Internationale"!

SIR CHARLES.    That's not "The Internationale," That's "99 Bottles of Beer on the Wall." *(We listen. He's right. Jane and Gertrude re-enter, Gertrude is pushing Miss Wilson.)*

JANE.    What's that off-key ruckus?

GERTRUDE.    The villagers, the villagers have come to kill us all!

JANE.    *(Overlapping.)* Sir Charles hold me!

GERTRUDE.    *(Overlapping.)* We're going to die!

SIR CHARLES.    *(Overlapping.)* Jane, grasp me, grasp me! *(Agatha cycles in, her eyes red and filled with raging tears.)*

SIDNEY.    Agatha! *(Agatha slaps Sidney.)* OW!

AGATHA.    Mr. Mengels, it has come to my attention that you are more directly connected to the Trefusis Affair than you have lead me to believed!

SIDNEY.    Miss Wylie, I can explain —

AGATHA.    Your familiarity with the Trefusis Family, your political leanings, and your behavior towards Mrs. Trefusis can mean only one thing: *YOU ARE THE KIDNAPPER OF SIDNEY TREFUSIS! (Erskine rushes on.)*

ERSKINE.    *(Points out front.)* LOOK!

ALL.    *WHAT*?

GERTRUDE.    It's Mrs. Trefusis!

JANE.    Leading the entire village straight through the green!

ERSKINE.    She's herding them like a Dresden shepherdess!

JANE.    Onto the school grounds —

GERTRUDE.    And right in our direction!

JANE and GERTRUDE.    MY WORD!

SIR CHARLES.    MY WALL!

MISS WILSON.    *MY FOUNDER'S DAY! (All rush off but Sidney and Lumpkin.)*

LUMPKIN.    *(To Sidney.)* Gonna be a helluva mess for you to clean up. *(The voices of "99 Bottles of Beer" roar up and cover the slow curtain.)*

## END OF ACT TWO

# ACT THREE

*The same.*

*Two hours later.*

*Bright red bricks are now strewn about the green. If possible, about 200 little red flags could be draped about too.*

*Since the disturbance, everything is a shambles.*

*A nice touch might include an upended baby carriage.*

*The mess should bring to mind a destroyed tea party or wedding.*

*And it should be fairly easy to clean up.*

*As lights rise, Sir Charles and Erskine are seated together on the grass downstage front. Erskine wears an academic gown over his wet suit. Sir Charles has put his jacket over his bathing trunks and looks suitably jaunty.*

*They share a bottle of champagne and are drunk.*

ERSKINE. All right, so tell me again: why did you call him "Sidders Smilash?"
SIR CHARLES. All very simple, really. Sidders because of Sidney, and "Smilash" because it's a compound of the words "Smile" and "Eyelash." His smile was always that boy's devilish best trait, and the eyelash, well, "soft 'ere was even his wickedest glance." A smile and an eyelash and Sidney Trefusis always had them running. Hence, his school-boy nickname: Sidders Smilash.
ERSKINE. And you didn't *recognize* him?

SIR CHARLES.     Blotted the fellow from my memory. When I heard he'd been 'napped by the Bolshies, I thought good riddance and rough for the Bolshies.

ERSKINE.     Extraordinary.

SIR CHARLES.     Always running around the school shouting "Marx and Engels! Marx and Engels!"

ERSKINE.     Hmmm. Wonder where he got "Mengels?"

SIR CHARLES.     Haven't the foggiest. D'ya think the women will ever come out of the Main House? It's hard to be so despised by so many of the bolder sex. Mrs. Trefusis is like an armada, Agatha won't speak to anybody, Jane won't speak to *me* now she knows I knew Mengels, and Gertrude Lindsay —

ERSKINE.     *(Moping.)* Gertrude Lindsay has *always* hated and despised me.

SIR CHARLES.     *(Perfectly rational.)* Not always. She's only known you since you met. *(Lumpkin enters, wheeling in Sidney, who is still chained to the tea table. Sidney sits atop the cart looking very miserable, his feet dangling like a petulant boy.)*

LUMPKIN.     *(As they enter.)* Sorry we weren't successful, sir.

SIDNEY.     How was I to know it was the wrong key. He's a *locksmith* for God's sake.

LUMPKIN.     *(To the others.)* It fit the latch to a public loo in Wilburn Crescent.

SIR CHARLES.     Say, Lumpers, no word from up top?

LUMPKIN.     Very secretive they've been in the Main House. Tell you true, it scares me. I've been handyman to this ladies' college for nigh on thirty years, and believe me true, there is nothing quite so frightening on this planet than a room full of eager, energetic young women who are at the same time so uncontrollably angry. *(Erskine begins to cry audibly. Sidney looks at him.)*

SIR CHARLES.     Mr. Erskine is in love with Gertrude Lindsay.

SIDNEY.     Oh.

SIR CHARLES.     Gertrude Lindsay is not in love with Mr. Erskine.

SIDNEY.     No kidding.

SIR CHARLES.     In the last three hours, Mr. Erskine has composed twelve bitter sonnets on the subject on unrequited love.

ERSKINE.    *(Dignified sniffling.)* I am enjoying my despair immensely.

SIDNEY.    *(To Sir Charles.)* I take it *you* are *not* in love with Gertrude Lindsay.

SIR CHARLES.    Only a *poet* could be in love with Gertrude Lindsay. I am in love with Jane Carpenter. When I think of her all I can see are stars and skies and starry skies.

SIDNEY.    Whenever you hear a man talking about stars and skies you may conclude that he is either an astronomer or a fool.

SIR CHARLES.    Ah, but Jane Carpenter and a fine, starry night would make a fool of any man.

ERSKINE.    *(Wailing.) I would be 'a fool for Gertrude Lindsay!*

SIDNEY.    At least you haven't far to go.

SIR CHARLES.    Have you that revolver, Trefusis? He pines for martyrdom.

SIDNEY.    If I had the revolver, do you think I'd still find myself chained to a tea cart? It was stomped under foot when that bloody mob crashed through here. Four hundred rabble shouting "GUILLOTINE! GUILLOTINE!" With *my wife* leading them out the gates.

LUMPKIN.    She saved the school though, sir.

SIDNEY.    Yes. "Property" was preserved.

SIR CHARLES.    Not *everyone's* property. You know, Trefusis, it has occured to me that this would be a fit occasion to rush forward and give you a bruised peeper!

SIDNEY.    You'd hit me because I had the villagers knock down your silly wall? You should thank me for making your wall part of history.

SIR CHARLES.    "History?" You tried to take over a charm school by armed occupation!

SIDNEY.    The ends justify the means.

SIR CHARLES.    'Specially if the ends are just as *bad* as the means.

SIDNEY.    Friends, we are all intelligent and/or educated men! If, like Lumpkin, not educated but intelligent; if like the two of you, not intelligent then educated. Surely we can recognize this system's time is up! It would be different if I saw some *hope* for the average working man in modern England, a workingman like — like Lumpkin here. But as it is, I am surrounded by battalions of millionaires and nary a Lumpkin in the bunch.

LUMPKIN.  That's true. Very few Lumpkins are millionaires.

SIDNEY.  We *all* have a stake in Socialism! I, the Revolutionary, because my sense of history tells me it *must* be. *(To Erskine.)* You, the Poet, because your sense of romance tells you it *should* be. *(To Lumpkin.)* You, the Worker, because your vested interest says it *shall* be. *(To Sir Charles.)* And you, the Aristocrat, because —

SIR CHARLES.  Well, because I can a*fford* to. *(Mr. Jansenius, blinking without his glasses and brandishing papers, enters. The binoculars are around his neck.)*

MR. JANSENIUS.  AH! *(Peering at Sidney through the binoculars.)* Sidney Trefusis it is indeed! Bewhiskered and shackled to a tea cart, just as I had been foretold! Pray, sir, do not *expound!*

SIDNEY.  Oh, lord, I'd forgotten how you spoke.

MR. JANSENIUS.  Trefusis, I have documents for you to sign. Terms of annulment between you and Mrs. Sidney Trefusis, nee Henrietta Jansenius.

SIDNEY.  You carry them *with* you?

MR. JANSENIUS.  For three months, in case you returned or I did meet you on a railway platform. *(Sidney throws down papers on the tea table.)*

SIDNEY.  And what if I've decided I *don't* want an annulment?

MR. JANSENIUS.  My daughter asks nothing of you in this agreement, villain. Not a thing — but *one* legal release.

SIDNEY.  And what is that one legal release?

MR. JANSENIUS.  That's for Henrietta to explain. In the meantime let me take this opportunity to challenge you to a duel.

SIDNEY.  Oh, no!

MR. JANSENIUS.  It's a question of honor, sir.

SIDNEY.  Tubby —

MR. JANSENIUS.  *(Embarrassed.) Sidney,* I-have-asked-you-a-thou-sand-times-not-to-*call*-me that!

SIDNEY. *(Moving away.)* Tubby, you're old as Methuselah, out of wind, and can't see the red in a Union Jack.

MR. JANSENIUS. Vengeance sharpens the vision!

SIDNEY. I'm over here, Tubby, you're talking to a chair.

MR. JANSENIUS. *(Confused.)* Oh! *(Mr. Jansenius raises his binoculars again to see Sidney.)* Where *are* you, you — ! *(Mr. Jansenius is peering straight at Lumpkin, who looks very uncomfortable. Mr. Jansenius removes the binoculars, squints, peers through them again.)* Good heavens! It's Lumpkin, isn't it?

LUMPKIN. *(Sheepish.)* Aye, sir, Mr. Jansenius, I was afeared what you should notice.

MR. JANSENIUS. This is the man I've searched the world over for thirty years!

SIDNEY. What are you talking about?

MR. JANSENIUS. When I made my first million in the South African diamond mines, I wondered aloud one day what to do with this sudden surge of kruggerands. I said it in my garden, a young man of sudden wealth in front of a young groundskeeper. "Where should I put my money?" I muttered. And he said: "PUT IT IN A TRUST."

SIDNEY. *HE* did?

LUMPKIN. *(Uncomfortable.)* Well —

MR. JANSENIUS. Precisely the words! And that's what I did, and without my knowledge of its doings, the Jansenius Trust has re-doubled our fortune every fortnight ever since.

SIR CHARLES. And so you rewarded Lumpkin's good advice?

MR. JANSENIUS. Jehovah, NO! I *SACKED* him! It was pure presumption! I still *took* the advice, of course, and after it paid off I regretted my haste and searched him out, but never heard a word! But, look here, Lumpkin, my *daughter* went to Alton College *and* Agatha, my ward. Why didn't you reveal yourself?

LUMPKIN. Well, sir, I didn't know as I'd given you *good* advice. I didn't even know you were speakin' of a *lot* of money. A million kruggerands is still three quid short of a pint as far as *I* know. Besides, I never said "*TRUST*."

MR. JANSENIUS. No?

SIDNEY.   Then what *did* you say?

LUMPKIN.   I said, "*TRUSS.*" Wear one myself to this very day. Keep a few quid hid away twixt girth and belt. If *you* heard "TRUST," well, happy day, but if that's the case your fortune's come way of a bad hernia. I didn't say "TRUST," sir.

MR. JANSENIUS.   But Lumpkin, I've put aside a small portion of the Jansenius fortune in hopes I'd someday find you!

LUMPKIN.   How small?

MR. JANSENIUS.   Two million pounds.

LUMPKIN.   (*Not a beat.*) Then I said, "TRUST," sir.

SIR CHARLES.   (*Toasting.*) Hooray for Lumpkin, Britain's newest millionaire! Where's your argument *now*, Trefusis? That must say *something* for a system that can produce such bounty in so short an exchange.

SIDNEY.   Of course it does, it says it's a ludicrous, hypocritical, and fatuously *stupid* bloody system! (*Beat.*)

LUMPKIN.   Be that as it may ...

SIDNEY.   There's no logic to a system that can produce immeasurable wealth because of bad hearing and a *hernia!*

LUMPKIN.   That's why I love this country.

MR. JANSENIUS.   Forgive my soon-to-be-former-son-in-law, regardless his financial portfolio, he has never had the true soul of a millionaire.

SIDNEY.   Look here, I may go about it badly, I may be a complete cock-up at revolution, but I'm not *WRONG!* Any book-keeper with half a brain can tally the injustice of this system, and any human being with two halves a heart can *feel* it even deeper.

SIR CHARLES.   Oh, you just want us to feel guilty.

SIDNEY.   Well, of *course* I do! When good men hang their heads collectively in shame, it's the first step towards ending the injustice! Tell me straight in the eye that a seven course meal at the most expensive restaurant in The Strand makes you feel better than bringing justice to a poor man's door. Is it *just* the mad Socialist who can see the blighted state of that poor man? Can't the Capitalist see him too?

MR. JANSENIUS.   Of *course* we can, Trefusis! We look at the same man — but we think different thoughts. A Socialist looks at that benighted fellow and says, "NO MAN SHOULD LIVE THAT WAY." A Capitalist sees the same man and says: "*I* SHALL NOT LIVE THAT WAY."

SIDNEY.    I never knew an aphorism could be so brutal.

MR. JANSENIUS.    It's not brutality, boy. Go ahead and change the world! Make it fair, make it just, you'll be in for a fight. But you won't make it happy.

SIDNEY.    *I don't care if it's happy!* Oh, the devil take this world! Blow it all up and start a conversation with the rubble!

ERSKINE.    "The soul of a millionaire."

SIDNEY.    What's that?

ERSKINE.    I was just thinking: Perhaps a man *should* have the soul of a millionaire. Wouldn't a millionaire's soul be full of bounty? And riches? And wondrous gifts to those you love? If we all had the souls of millionaires there'd be no need for revolution or Socialism. We'd all be infinitely generous because we'd feel we had infinite wealth at our disposal. A man could have that soul all his life and never a penny in the bank.

SIR CHARLES.    Good lord, a poet after all.

ERSKINE.    I'm not a poet, Sir Charles. Without Miss Lindsay, I'm just a fool who rhymes.

SIR CHARLES.    You know, Sidders, this whole business about the wall? I was going to knock it down myself anyway.

SIDNEY.    What?

SIR CHARLES.    Of course.

SIDNEY.    Then why in deuces did you build it?

SIR CHARLES.    Part of my father's will. Old sod wanted to make it harder on the whole village even *after* he was gone. So he insisted on the wall. I was duty bound to follow his wishes. Didn't specify how *long* I had to keep it up though.

SIDNEY.    *(Aghast.)* When were you going to knock it down?

SIR CHARLES.    Guy Fawkes Day, of course. Already had the invitations printed up. *(Sidney buries his head in his hands. Miss Wilson rolls on in her wheelchair. She has on travelling clothes and a carpet bag on her lap.)*

MISS WILSON.    WRECKAGE! WRECKAGE!

ERSKINE.    Miss Wilson!

SIR CHARLES.    Good gosh, Miss W., what's the buzz?

69

MISS WILSON.   I am a ruined woman!

ERSKINE.   But Headmistress!

MISS WILSON.   *Don't call me that!*

SIR CHARLES.   Why not?

MISS WILSON.   Because I am no longer headmistress of Alton College!

ERSKINE.   Why?

SIR CHARLES.   What's happened?

SIDNEY.   What's going on?

MISS WILSON.   Don't ask *me,* ask the fat-faced, self-satisfied smirk of the Jansenius Trust!

MR. JANSENIUS.   Now, Miss Wilson, your poor health —

MISS WILSON.   Oh, to hell with that! *(Miss Wilson gets up out of her wheelchair and stomps about.)* Alton College's Trustees have just agreed to a *purchase* of the school by the share-holders of the Jansenius Trust!

SIDNEY.   A purchase!

SIR CHARLES.   Good lord!

ERSKINE.   My word!

LUMPKIN.   How much?

MISS WILSON.   They paid ten times its market value! The Trustees *couldn't* say no! If you want any more answers, make an appointment with *the new headmistress!*

ERSKINE.   *(Overlapping.)* New — ?

SIR CHARLES.   *(Overlapping.)* New Head — *(From off:  The sound of women singing "Rule Britannia.")*

VOICES.   *(Off.)* "Rule, Britannia!
   Britannia, rules the waves!
   Britons never, never, never shall be slaves!"

*(Henrietta, brandishing her parasol like a riding crop, enters on the march, followed by Agatha, Jane, and Gertrude, all with parasols.)*

HENRIETTA.   Troops, halt! *(They stop, in formation.)* At ease! *(They each pop open a parasol and erect them to a pose of feminine perfection.)*

MR. JANSENIUS.   Everything finished, my dear?

HENRIETTA.   All's well that ends well, papa.

SIDNEY.   Henrietta, what have you done?

HENRIETTA.   First things first. Carpenter? Lindsay? *(Jane and*

*Gertrude step forward.)*

JANE.   *(Salutes.)* Yes, ma'am!

GERTRUDE.   *(Salutes.)* At your elbow, ma'am, *sir!*

HENRIETTA.   Jane Carpenter. Forgive Sir Charles Brandon for having once known the villain Sidney Trefusis. You are made for each other, Jane, accept his proposal and set a date. Never was marriage so much like a merger. Here is your shuttlecock. *(Henrietta hands Jane the "bird.")*

JANE.   Thank you, ma'am. Sir Charles, would you like to volley with me?

SIR CHARLES.   *(Dreamy-eyed.)* I'll return your thrusts, whiffle for whiffle. *(They exit hand in hand.)*

HENRIETTA.   Gertrude Lindsay. *Endure* Mr. Erskine. *(Gertrude tries to protest.)* I know. *(Gertrude tries to protest again.)* I know. But he loves you beyond measure, and it is unwise to squander the love of such a whopping great heart. *(Gertrude goes up to Erskine.)*

GERTRUDE.   Mr. Erskine, I am to give you the benefit of the doubt. *(Swallows.)* Pray, sir: read me your poetry. *(Erskine blinks, pats his pockets, but he doesn't have his sonnet. He looks at her lovingly.)*

ERSKINE.

> Of all the poetry I am versed in,
> None sound so sweet as Gertrude Erskine.

*(Gertrude's eyes widen with delight. She kisses Erksine ferociously, grabs his hand and yanks him offstage.)*

HENRIETTA.   Papa, you may escort Miss Wilson to the station. Like Napolean, she will be retiring to the sea. Unlike Napolean, she will be living with her widowed sister in Bournemouth.

MISS WILSON.   *(Bitterly.)* Able was I ere I saw Bournemouth.

MR. JANSENIUS.   *(Advancing.)* Miss Wilson — ? *(Lumpkin comes forward.)*

LUMPKIN.   *(Taking Miss Wilson's bag.)* Allow me, mum.

MISS WILSON.   *(Shocked.)* You? But you *hate* me, Lumpkin! We have always been adversaries, and this very day I tried to bargain you away to make a silly point and save my stupid ego!

LUMPKIN.   Aye, miss, you've made a hash of it, haven't you?

But, you see, when power changes, a conquering army always sees its vanquished foe to safe passage 'cross the frontier. One never knows if that wheel of fire will come round *your* way the *next* time.

MISS WILSON.   *(Moved.)* Lumpkin, you are worth a million!

LUMPKIN.   *(Takes her arm.)* You don't know the half of it. *(Miss Wilson and Lumpkin exit.)*

MR. JANSENIUS.   I'm off, my sweet. She'll see to you, Trefusis.

SIDNEY.   *(Confused.)* I thought we were going to duel.

MR. JANSENIUS.   We *are*. The floor of *commerce* is the Jansenius field of honor, and Henrietta is the weapon of our satisfaction. For myself, I have learned far too much this afternoon. It will take a great deal of effort to retrieve my former level of ignorance. Perhaps I shall go to my Men's Club. There's never an occasion I don't leave it less informed than when I went in. *(Mr. Jansenius exits.)*

HENRIETTA.   Well.

SIDNEY.   *(Eyeing Agatha.)* Need Agatha Wylie stay for this, Hetty?

HENRIETTA.   Agatha Wylie is the *point*, Sidney. The girl's in love with you, she might as well know everything.

SIDNEY.   *Do* you know everything, Agatha Wylie?

AGATHA.   *Plenty. (Agatha collapses her parasol and sets it aside. She looks at the mess. During the following, she <u>unobtrusively</u> begins to clean up some of the overturned furniture, straightening chairs, finally bringing the baby carriage back up on its wheels.)*

HENRIETTA.   Now, Sidney: Under the new regime of the Jansenius Trust, the school will retain the name of Alton College. Tradition is important. And, as it is the best known and most respected institution dedicated to the education of those women who will next become the — what was it, Agatha?

AGATHA.   "The consorts of cabinet ministers, captains of industry, and peers of the realm."

HENRIETTA.   Since we are to educate that generation of the female sex that will so determine the political future of Britain, it is important they learn the right lessons.

SIDNEY.   *(Sneers.)* By which you mean the teaching of table manners will proceed unhindered.

HENRIETTA.    Not so, Sidney. Alton College is going to become a serious institution of higher learning. We shall teach
the works of Hobbes, Burke, "The Wealth of Nations." In
short: everything you despise.

SIDNEY.    *(Rearing up.)* Very well, then! I'll contact the Trustees myself! The Trefusis Cotton Fortune is at least as powerful as the Jansenius Trust! I'll *outbid* you!

HENRIETTA.    *(Smiling.)* CAPITALIST!

SIDNEY.    Then — then I'll set up a competing school, just
the other side of the Thames. I'll teach my *own* history and
philosophy and — and —

HENRIETTA.    Free Love?

SIDNEY.    I'll teach Socialism!

HENRIETTA.    And I'll teach Capitalism, and we can com-
pete in the open marketplace of ideas. And you know what,
Sidney? Your school will attract the daughters of trade union-
ists, left-wing essayists, and vegetarians while *I* will continue to
recruit the consorts of kings.

SIDNEY.    *(Beat. He looks at her anew.)* Good Lord. Hetty —
You're beginning to sound like a Woman of Destiny.

HENRIETTA.    I believe papa gave you papers to sign? *(Agatha
picks them up from the tea table and hands them to Sidney, who locks
eyes with Agatha for a moment.)*

SIDNEY.    Ah yes, our annulment.

HENRIETTA.    The same.

SIDNEY.    Your father mentioned a certain legal release, Hetty.
What bargain must I make to free your name, hm? Every penny
I have?

HENRIETTA.    Not *things*, Sidney, not wealth or property. As
long as you agree to one demand.

SIDNEY.    Which is?

HENRIETTA.    I do not wish to free my name. After our annulment I wish to be known as "MRS. SIDNEY TREFUSIS." For
life.

SIDNEY.    But why?

HENRIETTA.    I am going to become very important in the
shaping of the future in Capitalist England. And I want that

future of Capitalism to be forever linked ... to *your name.*

SIDNEY. And if I refuse?

HENRIETTA. *Then I'll* take every penny you have.

SIDNEY. HA!

HENRIETTA. You laugh, but I know better, Sidney. You'd like to believe you could overthrow the government without a farthing, but as you've pointed out, you're both a millionaire and a Socialist, and this is a contradiction. Well, from what *I* can tell — the *purchased* disguise, the *purchased* handcuffs, the *purchased* march on Alton College — you're not much of a Socialist *unless* you're a millionaire! Besides, I believe you've exhausted all your currency with me.

SIDNEY. Are we talking love or politics?

HENRIETTA. Love and politics do not mix. I learned that when you broke my heart and left it smashed to dust.

SIDNEY. *(Tentatively.)* And ... what if I told you I was willing to ... pick up the pieces?

HENRIETTA. It won't work, Sidney. As Agatha said: marriage is an institution; you'd blow it up again.

SIDNEY. How do you *know?*

HENRIETTA. You're a revolutionary, it's what you *do.* The papers? *(Agatha hands Sidney a pen. He looks at her. She averts his glance. Sidney signs the paper.)*

SIDNEY. So, Hetty: you're now headmistress of Alton College, eh?

HENRIETTA. For heaven's sake, wherever did you get *that* idea?

SIDNEY. Well, I assumed when Miss Wilson —

HENRIETTA. Sidney, I'm just the absent proprietor. We *have* a *manager.* Agatha? *(Henrietta signals to Agatha. Agatha turns.)*

SIDNEY. But you can't! Agatha Wylie, you mustn't! This is what you meant about her heart and mind, wasn't it, Hetty?

HENRIETTA. She hasn't agreed *yet,* Sidney. Convince her not to, if you can, it's hers to choose.

SIDNEY. But, Hetty, she's 20 years old, she hasn't even graduated, she can't run a *school!*

HENRIETTA. It's *my* school!

SIDNEY. But —

HENRIETTA.   I bought it, I paid for it, it's mine.

SIDNEY.   Don't do it, Agatha! It'll break your spirit, a job like this!

HENRIETTA.   Nonsense, it will give her *steel* to grow up quite so fast! Grim responsibility is good for the soul! Women cannot afford to be so fragile in this world!

SIDNEY.   Agatha, you're too bright, too bold, too full of life! You're the Marxist Romantic! The Love Millionaire! You're —

HENRIETTA.   Decide, my dear.

SIDNEY.   Comrade Agatha! *(Beat.)*

AGATHA.   Headmistress Wylie, if you please. *(Sidney turns away.)*

HENRIETTA.   Don't be a glummy-puss, Sidney. The battle's not over yet. You're going to set up camp across the Thames, aren't you? It'll be fun to be at war for forty or fifty years. It's what married couples *do*, after all. Matter of fact, I've *enjoyed* this afternoon. To be quite honest, I've rather more enjoyed it than my wedding day. I may even marry again.

SIDNEY.   Marry? Whom?

HENRIETTA.   The Reverend Cosmo Prippit.

SIDNEY.   Oh, g-good G-God-God-God!

HENRIETTA.   He loves me, Sidney. And he has a good face. The Reverend Prippit has the kind of face one wants to see on one's deathbed.

SIDNEY.   As I'm sure so many often *do*.

HENRIETTA.   Don't be petulant, Sidney. That kind of thinking has brought great clarity to my life. To ask one's self whose face one wants to see when the days are almost over. I don't think I'd *want* to see *your* face, Sidney.

SIDNEY.   *(Stung.)* Well ... well, I don't want to see *your* face either!

HENRIETTA.   You don't?

SIDNEY.   NO! *(Scornful.)* "The face I want to see on my deathbed"! BOSH! I don't want to see your face on my *deathbed!* On my deathbed, I want to see the face of the best physician in Europe, the best nurse in England, and if I'm not completely past my life of atheism, the most lenient priest in Christendom! I don't want to see your face when I'm *dying!* I want to see your face in my life! At work and at rest and at morning and night, a face filled with fire and anger and wonder, filled with passion and delight, full of your heart and your soul and your mind and me! I DON'T WANT TO SEE YOUR FACE AT MY DEATH! I WANT TO SEE YOUR FACE IN MY *LIFE!* And I'm so *young*, Hetty. I'm going to live for such a *long* time without you.

HENRIETTA.   You love me.

SIDNEY.   A bit.

HENRIETTA.   *(Smiles kindly.)* Hurts, doesn't it? You see I did love you Sidney. The woman you called Hetty loved you so. But if you were loved *now* by the woman I've *become* ... it would be *alarming. (Beat.)* I'm leaving you. *(Henrietta exits. Sidney watches her disappear into the distance.)*

SIDNEY.   *(Ashes.)* Smashed to pieces. *(Sidney turns to Agatha.)*

AGATHA.   Did you know that the Spanish for both wife and handcuff are the same word? *"ESPOSA." (Agatha takes a large pin from her hat.)*

SIDNEY.   *(Pointing at the hatpin.)* A key!

AGATHA.   *(Deadpan.)* Oh, good, you *do* speak the language. *(Agatha goes to Sidney and begins working the lock.)* A ladies' hatpin is always the best locksmith.

SIDNEY.   Thank you, Headmistress. *(They are close together as Agatha fiddles with the handcuffs. After a slight beat.)*

AGATHA.   *(Working the lock.)* You know I don't love you anymore.

SIDNEY.   *(Nods.)* Not many people *do.*

AGATHA.   *(Won't look up at him.)* I don't *love* you. But — you're not *wrong* about things, Mr. Trefusis. You want so much from the world. It's just that the way you go *about* revolution I'm afraid all you do is break things.

SIDNEY.   Fine then! I'll give the whole thing up!

AGATHA.   Give up? Not a bit of it! You're going to start that school on the other side of the Thames! Spend your fortune, hire the best minds! It may take all your life or longer, but *much can be achieved by men and women who are not afraid of themselves — AND not in too much a hurry to see the harvest they have sown for!* Besides ... you'd have a comrade. *(Agatha has freed*

*Sidney.)*
SIDNEY.    "Comrade?" *(Sound of a girl's choir singing off.)* I say, what's that?
AGATHA.    My first official act as head of Alton College. The girls are burning the *My Faults* book in a bonfire — to the tune of a song I slipped into the Glee Club Hymnal.
SIDNEY.    *(Recognizing it.)* "The Internationale!"
AGATHA.    I told them it's from *Pirates of Penzance.*
SIDNEY.    But you're the new headmistress of the Capitalist gang.
AGATHA.    *(Shrugs.)* I could be a ... friend in power.
SIDNEY.    A *spy*? A secret agent deep within the system?
AGATHA.    There are *so* many ways of taking down a wall, Mr. Trefusis. You can smash your head against it ... or you can take it apart from the inside — brick by brick.
SIDNEY.    *(Admiringly.)* Damn!
AGATHA.    And I *should* tell you — regardless the new lack of affection I feel for you ... I *am* still *attracted* to you.
SIDNEY.    Are you, really? I'm a heartless man, Agatha Wylie. A reckless, brainless, romantic fool!
AGATHA.    *(Looks square at him.)* I know. Don't reform your-self *too* terribly quickly. *(Issuing an order.)* Right, now, look to the future: do you find *me* attractive?
SIDNEY.    *(Salutes.)* I find you so attractive you could be an-other man's wife.
AGATHA.    But you don't love me.
SIDNEY.    No, I don't *love* you. And you?
AGATHA.    Love *you*? Not a bit. *(Beat.)*
SIDNEY.    Good.
AGATHA.    Good. *(Beat.)*
SIDNEY.    *(Smiles.)* Then let's change the world! Before we do! *(Sidney smashes the champagne bottle. Immediately on the sound system: The Beatles singing "Revolution."\* Very loud.)*

## THE END


\* See Special Note on Songs and Recordings on copyright page.

# PROPERTY LIST

Bridal bouquet (HENRIETTA)
Red carpet bag (SIDNEY)
Champagne flutes (HENRIETTA)
Large book (JANE, GERTRUDE)
Lady's bicycle (AGATHA)
Unicycle or scooter or penny farthing bicycle (SIDNEY)
Necklace watch (MISS WILSON)
Croquet mallet (SIDNEY)
Whistle (MISS WILSON)
White chairs (LUMPKIN)
Small white table (LUMPKIN)
Tea table with tea service (LUMPKIN)
Binoculars (SIDNEY, MR. JANSENIUS)
Pocket watch (SIDNEY)
Map (SIDNEY)
Gun (revolver) (SIDNEY, AGATHA, LUMPKIN)
Handcuffs (SIDNEY, HENRIETTA)
2 pairs of eyeglasses (MR. JANSENIUS)
Bottle of champagne (ERSKINE, SIR CHARLES)
Annulment papers (MR. JANSENIUS, AGATHA)
Carpet bag (MISS WILSON)
Parasols (HENRIETTA, AGATHA, GERTRUDE, JANE)
Pen (AGATHA)
Hat pin (AGATHA)

# SOUND EFFECTS

Whistle
Bicycle bell

# NEW PLAYS

★ **THE CIDER HOUSE RULES, PARTS 1 & 2 by Peter Parnell, adapted from the novel by John Irving.** Spanning eight decades of American life, this adaptation from the Irving novel tells the story of Dr. Wilbur Larch, founder of the St. Cloud's, Maine orphanage and hospital, and of the complex father-son relationship he develops with the young orphan Homer Wells. "…luxurious digressions, confident pacing…an enterprise of scope and vigor…" *–NY Times.* "…The fact that I can't wait to see Part 2 only begins to suggest just how good it is…" *–NY Daily News.* "…engrossing…an odyssey that has only one major shortcoming: It comes to an end." *–Seattle Times.* "…outstanding…captures the humor, the humility…of Irving's 588-page novel…" *–Seattle Post-Intelligencer.* [9M, 10W, doubling, flexible casting] PART 1 ISBN: 0-8222-1725-2 PART 2 ISBN: 0-8222-1726-0

★ **TEN UNKNOWNS by Jon Robin Baitz.** An iconoclastic American painter in his seventies has his life turned upside down by an art dealer and his ex-boyfriend. "…breadth and complexity…a sweet and delicate harmony rises from the four cast members…Mr. Baitz is without peer among his contemporaries in creating dialogue that spontaneously conveys a character's social context and moral limitations…" *–NY Times.* "…darkly funny, brilliantly desperate comedy…TEN UNKNOWNS vibrates with vital voices." *–NY Post.* [3M, 1W] ISBN: 0-8222-1826-7

★ **BOOK OF DAYS by Lanford Wilson.** A small-town actress playing St. Joan struggles to expose a murder. "…[Wilson's] best work since *Fifth of July*…An intriguing, prismatic and thoroughly engrossing depiction of contemporary small-town life with a murder mystery at its core…a splendid evening of theater…" *–Variety.* "…fascinating…a densely populated, unpredictable little world." *–St. Louis Post-Dispatch.* [6M, 5W] ISBN: 0-8222-1767-8

★ **THE SYRINGA TREE by Pamela Gien.** Winner of the 2001 Obie Award. A breathtakingly beautiful tale of growing up white in apartheid South Africa. "Instantly engaging, exotic, complex, deeply shocking…a thoroughly persuasive transport to a time and a place…stun[s] with the power of a gut punch…" *–NY Times.* "Astonishing…affecting …[with] a dramatic and heartbreaking conclusion…A deceptive sweet simplicity haunts THE SYRINGA TREE…" *–A.P.* [1W (or flexible cast)] ISBN: 0-8222-1792-9

★ **COYOTE ON A FENCE by Bruce Graham.** An emotionally riveting look at capital punishment. "The language is as precise as it is profane, provoking both troubling thought and the occasional cheerful laugh…will change you a little before it lets go of you." *–Cincinnati CityBeat.* "…excellent theater in every way…" *–Philadelphia City Paper.* [3M, 1W] ISBN: 0-8222-1738-4.

★ **THE PLAY ABOUT THE BABY by Edward Albee.** Concerns a young couple who have just had a baby and the strange turn of events that transpire when they are visited by an older man and woman. "An invaluable self-portrait of sorts from one of the few genuinely great living American dramatists…rockets into that special corner of theater heaven where words shoot off like fireworks into dazzling patterns and hues." *–NY Times.* "An exhilarating, wicked…emotional terrorism." *–NY Newsday.* [2M, 2W] ISBN: 0-8222-1814-3

★ **FORCE CONTINUUM by Kia Corthron.** Tensions among black and white police officers and the neighborhoods they serve form the backdrop of this discomfiting look at life in the inner city. "The creator of this intense…new play is a singular voice among American playwrights…exceptionally eloquent…" *–NY Times.* "…a rich subject and a wise attitude." *–NY Post.* [6M, 2W, 1 boy] ISBN: 0-8222-1817-8

**DRAMATISTS PLAY SERVICE, INC.**
440 Park Avenue South, New York, NY 10016   212-683-8960   Fax 212-213-1539
postmaster@dramatists.com   www.dramatists.com